D1553927

The End of Sacrifice

The End of Sacrifice

Religious Transformations in Late Antiquity

GUY G. STROUMSA

Translated by Susan Emanuel

The University of Chicago Press ❃ *Chicago and London*

GUY G. STROUMSA is the Martin Buber Professor of Comparative Religion at the Hebrew University of Jerusalem. He is the author of, among other books, *Hidden Wisdom: Esoteric Traditions and the Roots of Christian Mysticism* (rev. ed. 2005) and *Barbarian Philosophy: The Religious Revolution of Early Christianity* (1999).

SUSAN EMANUEL has translated several books, most recently Aviad Kleinberg's *Seven Deadly Sins: A Very Partial List* (2008).

The University of Chicago Press, Chicago 60637
The University of Chicago Press, Ltd., London
© 2009 by The University of Chicago
All rights reserved. Published 2009
Printed in the United States of America
18 17 16 15 14 13 12 11 10 09   1 2 3 4 5

ISBN-13: 978-0-226-77738-2 (cloth)
ISBN-10: 0-226-77738-3 (cloth)

Originally published as *La Fin du sacrifice: Les mutations religieuses de l'Antiquité tardive.* © Odile Jacob, 2005.

Published with the support of the National Center for the Book—French Ministry of Culture.
Ouvrage publié avec le soutien du Centre national du livre—ministère français chargé de la culture.

Library of Congress Cataloging-in-Publication Data

Stroumsa, Guy G.
    [Fin du sacrifice. English]
    The end of sacrifice: religious transformations in late antiquity / Guy G. Stroumsa; translated by Susan Emanuel.
         p.   cm.
    Includes index.
    ISBN-13: 978-0-226-77738-2 (cloth: alk. paper)
    ISBN-10: 0-226-77738-3 (cloth: alk. paper) 1. Church history—Primitive and early church, ca. 30–600.
2. Rome—Civilization—Christian influences.
3. Sacrifice—Rome. 4. Christianity and other religions—Rome. 5. Rome—Religion. I. Title.
BR170.S8713   2009
261.2′2—dc22

                                                    2008026885

Contents

Foreword

We are always fascinated by what we do not know or, more exactly, by what is poorly understood. The religious transformations marking Late Antiquity belong to the kind of reality that arouses fascination. The attendance at the Collège de France by a broad audience that included colleagues and enlightened auditors at Guy Stroumsa's lectures is a perfect illustration of this fact. For who is still satisfied with the elementary dialectic of the Hegelian history of salvation?

How did the Greco-Roman world shift into Christianity? Since Budé, Gibbon, and Hegel, explanations that claim to resolve this enigma have not been lacking. But the oppositions between Christianity and "paganism" that fed the argumentation of the great theories have endured too long. Did the transformation result from a long and imperceptible evolution of the same reality? Weren't the ancient Christianities, all things considered, just an evolved "paganism"? Or are we dealing with a revolution that culminated after a few decades in the unforeseen demise of the ancestral religiosity of the Greeks and Romans? Or was it due to the attraction exercised by monotheism? But looked at closely, the Roman and Greek forms of worship always included an implicit or explicit discourse that aimed to define divine power as one single entity. Roman "polytheism," for example, always oscillated between two conceptions of divinity: as sole source of power and as reference point of a multitude of divinized powers and authorities. In this sense, what has been called by the name "polytheism" is in fact a religion that exposes the mystery of divine power without making a choice between a sole agent and the manifestations of its power. But Christianities did not neglect this problem either, as Hermann Usener stressed in his famous *Götternamen.*[1] Outside Judaism, strictly monotheistic religions were rare in Antiquity. One cannot oppose ancestral religions to Christianity as ritual religions contrasted to a spiritual religion. Ritualistic religions do not in any way ignore spirituality, just as Judaism and Christianity never rejected ritual obligations. So should we contrast a civic religion, linked to the legal status of the individual, to religions that implied a personal choice? But non-Christians also made a choice when they committed themselves to philosophical sects or to certain mystery cults, which did not suffice to make them adversaries of traditional religions. And so the debates continue.

In the last generation, religious transformations specific to Late Antiquity have produced an avalanche of books and studies without anyone arriving at a convincing solution. Nevertheless, a certain amount of important progress has been made. This is why it seemed interesting to ask one of the authorities in the debate to present the advances and try to make a provisional assessment. Guy Stroumsa was kind enough to accept the invitation to explain to us his thinking on the mystery of the conversion of the ancient world. For me, he succeeded in making a synthesis of the theory of imperceptible evolution and the theory of a determining historical event.

Guy Stroumsa demonstrates that the abolition of sacrifice, that central act of ancestral piety, undeniably represents the crucial moment of the transformations—among the Greeks and Romans, of course, but especially and brutally among the Jews. The

---

1. Hermann Usener, *Götternamen: Versuch einer Lehre von der religiösen Begriffs-bildung* (1896; repr., Frankfurt: Schulte-Bulmke, 1948).

latter had been forced by the destruction of the Temple in 70 CE to invent a new Jewish religion. Imperceptibly, while conserving and commenting upon the norms that characterized them, the Jews no longer offered sacrifice in a temple. Temptations of this type had a history in the Israel of the Second Temple, but everything was accelerated by the intervention of the Roman legions. Guy Stroumsa invites us to see this historic event, arising in the very framework of Judaism, as one of the central (and often forgotten) elements of the transformations that would be produced in the course of the following centuries. In adding Judaism to the arguments of the debate, Stroumsa incontestably opens new perspectives. He draws our attention to the fact that under the impetus of Judaism and its problems, it was foremost the Oriental religious landscape that was transformed, before the transformations went on to affect the whole of the *oikoumenē*. The reader perceives that Christianity merits the name "Oriental religion"— much more so than the forms of religiosity that Franz Cumont (in his lectures at the Collège de France a century ago) placed at the center of religious transformations. In contrast, profoundly anchored as they were in the traditional religions of the ancient world, the cults of Isis or the Sibyl would never have been able to capture minds and the world as did Christianity under the influence of Judaism.

This religion deprived of sacrifice—or rather, which replaced sacrifice by other forms of devotion—was a piety that inserted various elements of wisdom and Greco-Roman culture into a new framework and chose in exclusive fashion a single interpretation of the divine mystery. The end of sacrifice indeed constitutes a decisive element that is found at the center of the religious transformations of Late Antiquity, which Stroumsa enables us to see in a way that is both vibrant and fascinating.

John Scheid, Collège de France, 2005

Preface

Non uno itinere perveniri potest ad tam grande secretum.
(Such a great secret is not attainable by a single path.)
«SYMMACHUS, *Relatio* 3.10»

This book has its proximate origin in four lectures given at the
Collège de France in February 2004, but its distant roots are
more difficult to discern. It has now been for more than twenty
years that the profound transformations of the very concept of
religion under the Roman Empire have occupied and preoccupied me. I have even spoken of the "religious revolution" to
describe some of the specific traits of ancient Christianity. The
many references to my own work in the pages that follow reflect
the continuity of some aspects of my research, of which I present
here a sort of synthetic vision. I have worked as a historian of religions on movements that were sometimes radical or marginal,
such as some of the currents called "Gnostic," or on religions that
are often marginalized by too many scholars thinking about *Antike und Christentum*, such as Manichaeism or rabbinic Judaism.
I believe I have tried to detect (via different avenues) some of the
moving boundaries of religious geography in the Mediterranean
and Near Eastern world around the end of the ancient period
(roughly speaking, from Jesus to Muhammad).

I am fully aware that my groping research belongs in the framework of the impressive advances made in many places for the past generation in our appreciation of the religious phenomena of Late Antiquity and their complexity. Since Fernand Braudel and Shlomo Dov Goitein, the Mediterranean is in fashion. From archaeology to anthropology, researchers are speculating about the profound unity, hidden or fictive, of diverse phenomena that are observed in various societies of the Mediterranean world. With regard to religious phenomena, in our period as in others, we would be starting off on the wrong path if we postulated a Mediterranean identity running from the most distant antiquity to our day. Such a postulate would obscure the central role of the Near East. Here, of course, I am literally preaching *pro domo*. Living in Israel, I feel myself at the very mainspring where the Mediterranean and the Near East connect. What might appear to some as an advantage for scholarly observation is certainly not without a terrible price, of which the newspapers and television remind us every day. To the misleading dichotomy between Mediterranean and Near East is added another that is no less dangerous: that between polytheistic and monotheistic religions. Of course there are differences, often fundamental ones, among the various religions that lived in contact (and in conflict) with one another in waning Antiquity. But the most essential of these differences are not necessarily those reflected in the pantheons, but rather anthropological conceptions and ethical attitudes that are sometimes much sharper or deeper. Whatever the case, in their diverse religious identities, societies of both the Near East and those of Europe are heirs (sometimes distant ones) of the new configurations taking shape in Late Antiquity, which were then structured in various medieval societies. Thus, to reflect on the religious transformations of Late Antiquity means also to distance oneself in order to observe the deep roots of some of the problems, sometimes urgent and serious, with which we are confronted today.

The terms of the French invitation imposed the form: I was asked to give four lectures, and so I had to define four fundamental articulations that reflect what I have called the "religious transformations" of Late Antiquity. It would certainly have been possible to identify other transformations. What matters in any scholarly essay is to avoid both teleological and ideological approaches that identify a single transcendent factor that is supposed to explain something, and also to avoid generalizing, which prevents recognizing the great lines of evolution. Perhaps it is worth noting here that in Bruce Lincoln's study of the shift from the religions of the ancient world to those of the "post-ancient" world, he identifies four essential domains, too: discourse, practice, community, and institution.[1]

To give four lectures, each to be read rather quickly in sixty minutes, is to impose on oneself, at best, a considerable challenge. This challenge becomes a threat if one must speak in a language that one has not used daily for a long time, in a large hall filled with a diverse audience comprising both general (but eager and curious) listeners from the public, as well as colleagues who want specific historical and philological arguments. One has to say something on each occasion that is new to everybody, without being either too technical or too rhetorical. I was asked to publish these lectures as they had been given orally. The four first chapters of this book represent the texts of the lectures, almost untouched. I have added as a fifth chapter a paper that has previously been published, but which seems to contribute naturally to the general argument of this book. There was no question of adding scholarly and technical notes to these non-technical texts aimed at a wide and informed public. Therefore, the notes included here are meant only to orient research, support assertions, or help to lay out my reasoning. The reader may recognize from these indications the contours (and limits) of my knowledge. He or she can easily take account of the field's changes in perspective due to differences in scholarly culture and intellectual approach.

It is to the warm friendship of John Scheid that I owe the

---

1. Bruce Lincoln, "Epilogue," in *Religions of the Ancient World: A Guide*, ed. Sarah I. Johnston (Cambridge, MA: Harvard University Press, 2004), 657–67.

invitation to give these lectures. I hope I have not disappointed him, nor my friends and teachers who did me the honor of coming to hear me, and who so kindly welcomed my wife and me to Paris. I thank them all and in particular Nicole Belayche, who willingly read the text of these lectures and made many judicious remarks. In any case, I found great and unexpected pleasure in writing these essays in French. I also want to thank the Fondation Hugot of the Collège de France that housed us during our stay in Paris in exceptional comfort.

During the 2003 autumn semester, I presented and discussed the essence of these lectures, with primary texts, in my graduate seminar. I thank my students, and in particular Jonathan Moss and Tali Artman, for their great curiosity and intellectual vivacity. The exceptional working conditions granted by the Scholion Center of the Hebrew University in Jerusalem allowed me to write this book rather quickly. I also want to express my gratitude to Sharon Weisser for having reread, accented, and corrected the French manuscript on her "azerty" keyboarded computer.

>>><<<

I dedicate this book to the memory of my parents-in-law. Zoshka Wallach, née Ludmer, grew up in Maniava, a village in Ukrainian Poland. Throughout her life she kept the vivid memory of the religious hatred that marked her childhood. Zvi Wallach knew from the Cernowitz of his youth about the stakes of cultural encounters and transformations; he loved nothing more than to reflect on these stakes, these transformations and the modes they took across the history of peoples and cultures. Both opened to me in Jerusalem their home and their hearts.

Jerusalem, January 2005

Preface to the American Edition

The text of this book follows that of the French original, *La fin du sacrifice: Les mutations religieuses de l'antiquité tardive*, which was published in 2005. I have added some bibliographical references and corrected some mistakes, but have decided against the elaboration of a highly condensed argument that was originally presented orally.[1] That would have meant writing another book altogether. One significant change lies in the book's subtitle: in English, the semantic field of *mutations* is not equivalent to that of the French word. In particular, in English *mutations* implies a lack of agency that I certainly do not mean to emphasize. I have decided, therefore, to speak of *transformations*.

In the spring of 2006, the publication of the Gnostic *Gospel of Judas*, orchestrated by the *National Geographic*, highlighted the importance of polemics about sacrifices in earliest Christianity. In this text Jesus tells his disciples to "stop sacrificing," and the context seems to indicate that Jesus accuses bishops who support

---

1. The present publication has benefited from suggestions made in the wake of the Italian edition, Guy G. Stroumsa, *La fine del sacrificio: Le mutazioni religiose della tarda antichità* (Turin: Einaudi, 2006), xiv. I am deeply indebted to Giovanni Filoramo, Lorenzo Perrone, and Mauro Pesce for this publication.

martyrdom of condoning human sacrifice. There is no doubt that the newly available text will spur fresh research on the status of sacrifice in early Christian discourse. Although I cannot enter the scholarly discussion here, I am aware of the fact that some of the main claims of the present book bear directly on it.

This book is an attempt to suggest some of the main vectors of the radical and multifaceted transformation of religion in Late Antiquity. I make no claim to have identified all these vectors or to have dealt in depth with any of them. Like all major historical phenomena, this structural transformation was overdetermined. The emergence and eventual victory of Christianity clearly had a major impact upon the transformation of religious structures in the empire. Yet some patterns of religious change in the Roman Empire can already be detected within the polytheist system, as has been argued quite convincingly in recent years.[2] My thesis here, that Judaism may be perceived as the laboratory in which these structural changes occurred first, should be seen as complementary to other attempts to explain this paradigmatic shift in the history of religions.

The title, *The End of Sacrifice*, obviously a synecdoche, reflects the undeniable fact that animal sacrifices—"the quintessential ritual complex of ancient civilizations," in Fritz Graf's words— are precisely what disappears from ritual ubiquity in Late Antiquity, in the Near East as well as around the Mediterranean.

For many American scholars, continuity in Late Antiquity religious history, "at the broadest level," seems to be more sig-

---

2. See in particular Jörg Rüpke, "Patterns of Religious Change in the Roman Empire," in *The Changing Face of Judaism, Christianity, and Other Greco-Roman Religions in Antiquity*, ed. Ian H. Henderson and Gerbern S. Oegema (Studien zu den Jüdischen Schriften aus hellenistisch-römischer Zeit, 2; Gütersloh: Gütersloher Verlagshaus, 2006), 13–33; and James B. Rives, "Epilogue: Religious Change in the Roman Empire," in *Religion in the Roman Empire* (Oxford: Blackwell, 2007), 202–10. For another highly suggestive attempt at tracing major trajectories for the transformation of religion in antiquity, see Jonathan Z. Smith, "Here, There, and Anywhere," reprinted in J. Z. Smith, *Relating Religion: Essays in the Study of Religion* (Chicago: University of Chicago Press, 2004), 323–39.

nificant, or more interesting, than shifts, which are considered to have taken place only at the "intermediate level." Scholars involved in the social analysis of religion are prone to question the legitimacy, or at least the central status, of intellectual trends. For them, spiritualization and abstractions are not really characteristic of local "popular" culture and religion, where traditional patterns are very slow to die. The reaction against various forms of teleology, in particular against older Protestant models of the rise of introspective conscience, is certainly legitimate. It does not bear, however, upon my own argument, which seeks to take seriously the religious revolution of Late Antiquity. As a historian of religions, I believe in the capital importance of ideas and in the agency of beliefs (or rather of persons moved by their beliefs). As much as rituals, ideas provided the motor of religious transformation in Late Antiquity.

Some readers have been intrigued by the relative neglect in my argument of the Late Antiquity confrontation between polytheism and monotheism. To the extent that such neglect exists, it is a benign one, amounting to no implicit "demotion" of Hellenism. I can only repeat that perspective cannot be eliminated in the historical study of religion, and that a book on the spiritual roots of Europe, written in Jerusalem and originally meant for a Parisian audience, should not be identical to one written in Athens, or in Chicago.

A number of colleagues and friends have reacted, in print or orally, to the ideas presented here. I am grateful to all and would like in particular to mention my debt to Glen W. Bowersock, Rémi Brague, Jan N. Bremmer, Peter Brown, David Frankfurter, Winrich Löhr, Francesca Prescendi, Maurice Sartre, and Paul Veyne. I should also like to thank Brian Stock, who was instrumental in bringing the French original to the attention of the Press; Alan Thomas and Erin DeWitt, from the University of Chicago Press, and Susan Emanuel, who translated the text with great enthusiasm. I acknowledge the permission granted by Indiana University Press to republish here, as chapter 5, a piece that originally appeared in David Brakke, Michael L. Satlow, and Steven Weitzman, eds., *Religion and the Self in Antiquity* (Bloomington: Indiana University Press, 2005), 183–96.

Jerusalem, May 2008

1

A New Care of the Self

Guillaume Budé, who suggested to François I that a Parisian equivalent of the Collegium Trilingue in Louvain be created, published in 1534 a large volume on "the shift from Hellenism to Christianity," *De transitu Hellenismi ad Christianismum.*[1] *'Ellēnismos*, a term borrowed from Clement of Alexandria and Gregory of Nazianzus, meant for him what the New Testament calls "the world." Budé wanted to understand and explain to a knowledgeable and enlightened readership the essential workings of a profound transformation in the religious identity in the Mediterranean world under the Roman Empire. From Marcus Aurelius to Augustine, one can in effect follow the Christianization of subjectivity, of anthropology, of the emotions, along with the Christianization of structures of thought and of religious practice. More profoundly, it seems to be the very definition of religion, as well as its dialectical relations with society, that emerges transformed

1. Guillaume Budé, *Le passage de l'hellénisme au christianisme—De transitu Hellenismi ad Christianismum,* trans. and ed. Marie de la Garanderie and Daniel F. Penham (Paris: Les Belles Lettres, 1993). On Budé's humanist project, see Jean Plattard, *Guillaume Budé (1468–1540) et les origines de l'humanisme français* (Paris, 1923; repr., Paris: Les Belles Lettres, 1966), 28–31.

in a radical way toward the end of Late Antiquity—thus heralding the medieval cultures in their three essential forms, those of
Byzantium and of Islam alongside that of the Latin West. The
religious transformations of the Mediterranean and Near Eastern world in the first centuries of the Roman Empire are so radical that one may speak of *mutations*, using a term derived from
biology in a metaphorical way. I should right away justify using
a metaphor that might seem implicitly to suppress human actions and intentionality. On the contrary, it is evident that changes
(even the most dramatic and revolutionary) in human societies do
not occur as if by magic, but rather are due to actions, decisions,
and reflections that are both conscious and voluntary on the part
of individuals and collectivities. But these human decisions, specific and individual, are never sufficient, even in their sum, to explain the transformation as a whole. In other words, referring to
a concept familiar to us from Thomas Kuhn's epistemology of
the sciences, we are witnessing a "paradigm shift" in the domain
of the religious under the Roman Empire. If one has to specify in
a single word the nature of this change, I would accept the Hegelian analysis that stresses the *interiorization* of religion, even if
this means seriously qualifying the use of that term.[2]

Since Budé, this fundamental issue has been constantly re-
stated, taken up a thousand times from different angles, sometimes with fresh illumination, yet without establishing answers
that seem totally satisfactory, despite all the progress in historical thinking, in philology and archaeology, which have taught us
that matters were extremely complex. With regard to our present subject, we have learned that neither "paganism" nor even
"Christianity" can be reduced to a factitious unity that represents
anything. The forms of Christian existence in the first centuries
are numerous—and the concept of "paganism" is of course only
the creation of Christian thinkers and does not correspond to

2. See Guy G. Stroumsa, "Interiorization and Intolerance in Early Christianity," in
Die Erfindung des inneren Menschen, ed. Jan Assmann, Studien zum Verstehen fremder
Religionen, no. 6 (Gütersloh: Gütersloher Verlagshaus G. Mohn, 1993), 168–82.

any concrete reality. Here at the Collège de France, Pierre Hadot and Michel Foucault have offered reflections of great fecundity on this "shift" and its dramatic consequences.[3] If today I propose to take up the question once more, I also wish to pay homage to these two great names. To attack head-on such vast and funda-mental questions—especially when the time available requires me to make assertions (at best half-true ones) without really be-ing able to demonstrate them—is to risk failure, as I am only too aware. But in the Republic of Letters, a little audacity seems to be a duty.

The transformations that one observes across the *longue du-rée* of the Roman Empire (for which I use the fashionable term "Late Antiquity" in perhaps an overly loose way because I make it start very early, in the second rather than the fourth century) are certainly not all of a religious nature. But starting with Al-brecht Dieterich before the end of the nineteenth century, via Henri-Irénée Marrou and Eric Robertson Dodds, to Peter Brown and Robin Lane Fox, all historians interested in religious phe-nomena have not hesitated to speak of a new religiosity or piety, even a religious revolution, that sets in during the third century to assert itself during the fourth.[4] On this point, Peter Brown

3. See in particular Pierre Hadot's "Exercices spirituels," *Annuaire de la Ve section de l'École pratique des hautes études* 84 (1997): 25–70; reprinted in Pierre Hadot, *Exer-cices spirituels et philosophie antique*, 2nd ed. (Paris: Études augustiniennes, 2002), 19–74. See also in the same volume, "Un dialogue interrompu avec Michel Foucault: Conver-gences et divergences," 313–19. By Foucault, see in particular *The Hermeneutics of the Subject: Lectures at the Collège de France, 1981–1982*, trans. Graham Burchell (New York: Palgrave-Macmillan, 2005).

4. Henri-Irenée Marrou, *Décadence romaine ou Antiquité tardive? IIIe–IVe siècle* (Paris: Seuil, 1977). For Marrou, the new religiosity constitutes the essential originality of Late Antiquity. E. R. Dodds, *Pagan and Christian in an Age of Anxiety: Some Aspects of Religious Experience from Marcus Aurelius to Constantine* (Cambridge: Cambridge University Press, 1965). Robin Lane Fox, *Pagans and Christians* (Harmondsworth, UK: Penguin, 1986). See also the fine analyses of Peter Garnsey and Caroline Humfress, *The Evolution of the Late Antique World* (Cambridge: Cambridge University Press, 2001). For a serial analysis of Late Antiquity Christianization, see the important works of Ramsay MacMullen, *Christianizing the Roman Empire* (New Haven, CT: Yale Univer-sity Press, 1984); and *Christianity and Paganism in the Fourth to Eighth Centuries* (New Haven, CT: Yale University Press, 1997).

states flatly: "We live in a world where it is imperative that we should learn to understand revolutions."[5] It is a religious revolution because we are witnessing the crumbling of the ancient systems of the Greeks and Romans, but also that of Israel, founded as it was on daily sacrifices at the Temple of Jerusalem. Of all these religious systems, Judaism alone survived and was able to reconstitute itself, but at the price of radical transformations. If it was able to do so, this was undoubtedly because it found within itself, more so than did polytheistic systems, an implicit medium of change, the leaven of interiorization. And yet Judaism remains all too often absent from studies of the religious transformations of Late Antiquity. Dieterich remains typical in this respect: in his "Der Untergang der antiken Religion," dating from 1892, one finds not a word on Judaism.[6] This absence—due no doubt in large part, but not solely, to difficulties of a linguistic order—seems to me to prevent real understanding of these transformations.

Questions linked to religion and to religious identity that were previously thought to be settled, or nearly so (with the naïveté too often manifested by the master thinkers of the twentieth century), are today being reasserted, often in a stark and conflictual way. But in an era so troubled as ours, humanist and secular thought about the religious transformations at the very basis of our societies not only is not superfluous, but even appears with a new urgency.

I need to make a methodological point. The history of religions, as we know, has an ambiguous status. A science born of theology, by contrasting itself to the latter, finds it difficult to completely disengage from it. In my case, I will be studying dead and living religions together, some of which are our own or those of contemporary societies and, alas, sometimes still in conflict

---

5. Peter Brown, "Brave Old World," review of *Pagans and Christians* by Robin Lane Fox, *New York Review of Books* 34, no. 4 (March 12, 1987): 27.

6. Albrecht Dieterich, "Der Untergang der antiken Religion" (1892), in *Kleine Schriften* (Berlin: Teubner, 1911), 449–539.

with each other. Neither infatuation nor disdain nor unacknowl-edged polemic is acceptable. As a principle of method, I there-fore propose to study dead religions as if they were alive, and the living ones as if they were dead. The death of the former might help us to better understand the life of the latter, and vice versa.

The shift that interests us here is not simply from one religion to another, from paganism to Christianity, as it was formerly ex-pressed, or even from polytheistic to monotheistic systems, to use terms more in vogue today. Yet I am indeed fearful that these modern concepts ("polytheism" and "monotheism" date from the seventeenth century) do not always reflect entities or historical realities that are clearly defined, and especially so in the period that concerns us. Whatever the case, I am not sure that this heu-ristic principle is very useful for understanding the nature of the transformations that we are trying to observe. For example, the Platonist Celsus seems to be more strictly monotheistic than the Christian Origen.[7] Moreover, it seems to me that the predi-lection for both these terms, "polytheism" as well as "monothe-ism," reflects or sometimes hides apologetic or polemic attitudes that one does not dare to display in our societies, where religion and secularism remain in conflict, whether muffled or shrill.

The German philosopher Karl Jaspers characterized the first half millennium before our common era as an *Achsenzeit* (axial age), when across different (often imperial) civilizations there developed a hierarchical differentiation between the visible and invisible, the material and spiritual, worlds. Confucius, Buddha, Zarathustra, the prophets of Israel, and the first Greek philoso-phers represented for Jaspers the types of this intellectual and

---

7. On the stakes of the polemic between Celsus and Origen, see Guy G. Stroumsa, *Barbarian Philosophy: The Religious Revolution of Early Christianity*, Wissenschaft-liche Untersuchungen zum Neuen Testament, no. 112 (Tübingen: Mohr Siebeck 1999), 44–56. The non-pertinence of an opposition between the concepts of monotheism and polytheism to understand these religious transformations of Late Antiquity is discussed by Philippe Borgeaud in *Aux origines de l'histoire des religions* (Paris: Seuil, 2003).

religious transformation.[8] It seems to me that the era and domain we are studying also has a claim to this title of "axial age," an epoch in which the very frameworks of a civilization are transformed in a radical way. I would like to try to show how one may follow, roughly from Jesus to Muhammad, the transformation of the very concept of religion. In a sense, then, the conversion of Constantine and the Christianization of the empire permitted the establishment of a new sort of religion that was unknown in the ancient world. To a great extent, the religious transformations of Late Antiquity mark the foundation of European culture.[9]

The victory of Christianity in the Roman Empire risks distorting the way the problem is posed. Marrou wondered whether we should speak of "Low Empire" or "Late Antiquity." In our case, we might ask whether we are dealing with ancient Christianity or else Late Antiquity. In other words, are we not faced, in the Roman Empire of the second to the end of the fourth century, with transformations of societies and of the *Zeitgeist*—of which the religious transformations that may be observed are merely the consequences? Are the religious ideas of Christians the source of the observed transformations, or should we say that the Christians, more so (or better) than other religious groups, were able to make use of the new conditions offered by a culture in transformation? Without denying the dialectic between religion and culture, I support the idea that these transformations were above all religious in nature.

Despite the inclusion of Hebrew alongside Greek and Latin by the humanists within the educational curriculum at the beginning of the modern era, it seems that many scholars still forget or minimize the contribution and impact of ancient Judaism within our equation. Thus, the "shift from paganism to Christianity" is too often conceived, or at least perceived, as an inter-

8. For a new analysis of Jasper's thesis, see Shmuel Noah Eisenstadt, ed., *The Origin and Diversity of Axial Age Civilizations* (Albany: State University of New York Press, 1986).

9. See the first half of Daniel Dubuisson, *L'Occident et la religion: Mythes, science et idéologie* (Brussels: Éditions Complexe, 1998).

nal transformation, whether it is considered as beneficial or ill-fated. One will allow the Jerusalemite that I am to present things by taking into account both Judaism as an essential piece of our subject and Christianity as an Eastern religion, in its sources as well as in some of its developments. Christianity, a religion coming from the Near East to conquer Europe, has also remained until our day a religion of the Orient, from Ethiopia to Armenia.[10] In one of his last articles, Arnaldo Momigliano speculated about the simultaneous religious sentiments in Jerusalem, Athens, and in Rome in the first century BCE. Momigliano was clearly aware that the integration of Judaism into our equation might help to resolve the question of the essentially religious nature of the major transformations during our period.[11]

In chapter 2, I deal with the idea of a "religion of the Book" by trying to show the development during our period not only of this concept, but more profoundly of a new type of religion founded on revealed writing (or set of writings). Chapter 3 explores the deep transformation in the very idea of religious practice with the end of public blood sacrifices in the various religious systems of Late Antiquity and with the reconstitution of religious rituals on other bases. Chapter 4 discusses the new emphasis put on communitarian religion, of a community established voluntarily by individuals around a common faith, and the consequences of this transformation for interreligious relations (rather than the civic religion) functioning at the very heart of the city (or the state). Let me stress right away that this is more a change of emphasis than either a dichotomy or a linear progression, since religious communities had coexisted with the civic

---

10. See, for example, Micheline Albert et al., *Christianismes orientaux: Introduction à l'étude des langues et des littératures* (Paris: Cerf, 1993).

11. Arnaldo Momigliano, "Religion in Athens, Rome, and Jerusalem in the First Century B.C.," in *On Pagans, Jews, and Christians* (Middletown, CT: Wesleyan University Press, 1978), 74–91. On Momigliano as historian of religions, see Guy G. Stroumsa, "Arnaldo Momigliano and the History of Religions," in *Momigliano and Antiquarianism: Foundations of the Modern Cultural Sciences*, ed. Peter N. Miller (Toronto: University of Toronto Press, 2007), 28–311.

religious system since the Greek period. My pressing need to schematize and to cover long durations means running the great and almost inevitable risk of excessive generalization and simplification, a risk to which I have perhaps succumbed. Yet I hope I have succeeded, here and there, in discerning vectors and trajectories and in freshly illuminating certain essential questions.

In the course of the first stage of this overview, we will study a profound psychological transformation, perhaps the most profound psychological transformation in the history of the West. I am alluding to the shift of the center of gravity from the human person, from the subject, from life in this world, to the growing interest in the future of the person after death. Such a shift evidently must have had deep consequences for the implicit structures of religion, if not also for its explicit structures, by proposing a new construction of identity.

About eighty years ago, Gilbert Murray thought he had discerned in late paganism a "failure of nerve" of Greek religion, heralding its demise.[12] In his wake, E. R. Dodds proposed in *Pagan and Christian in an Age of Anxiety* (a book conceived and written at the beginning of the 1960s, amid great fear of nuclear war) a psychological and psychologizing analysis of religious experience (like William James's) under the Roman Empire. "Where did all this madness come from?" asks Dodds, referring to the exploits of Christian ascetics.[13] I would like to follow another path here, putting the accent on the impact of beliefs and practices on the structures of personality, rather than on the psychology, even a historicized one, of religion.

The new importance of individual eschatology, of the fate of the person after death, has less to do with the idea of the eternity of the soul (already central for Plato) than with the idea of the resurrection of the body and the Last Judgment. As we know, this is an idea that came from Iran and passed from there to

---

12. Gilbert Murray, *Five Stages of Greek Religion* (Garden City, NY: Doubleday, 1955).

13. Dodds, *Pagan and Christian in an Age of Anxiety*, 34.

Judaism, and from the latter into early Christianity.[14] This was also one of the characteristics of Christianity that would repel intellectual pagans the most. Judgment obliged each person to invest in his postmortem future rather than in the present. In a sense, the famous wager—whose attribution to Pascal often makes us forget its many antecedents, from Augustine to al-Ghazālī—was already present, in an implicit fashion, among Christianized Romans.

The very idea of a wager shows the new importance of both the reflexivity and radical seriousness of religious thought. Of course, theology as reflection on the gods is not a monotheistic idea. But the acceptance by Philo, the last representative of the Alexandrian Jewish tradition, of the Greek intellectual tradition and its application to the Bible, or "barbarian philosophy," opens a new era, at least until Spinoza. Reflexive thinking about religion—on myths as well as on practices—would now become an integral part of religion instead of remaining outside it.[15] Jewish theology, then Christian and Muslim theology, allows philosophy to study the myths and rites from both inside and outside. This new reflexivity is well-known, yet we have not finished interpreting its consequences—far from it. The German Egyptologist Jan Assmann, speaking in his book *Moses the Egyptian* about the essential difference between the monotheisms of Israel and Akhenaten, relies on what he calls "the Mosaic distinction," that is to say, the requirement of truth in religion, a requirement that is found nowhere else in the ancient world.[16] Such a requirement of truth, equivalent to a new status for truth, traverses all of ancient Christian thought, from the idea of *verus Israel* and that

14. For a history of the concept until the late Middle Ages, see Caroline Walker Bynum, *The Resurrection of the Body in Western Christianity, 200–1336* (New York: Columbia University Press, 1995). See also Jan N. Bremmer, *The Rise and Fall of the Afterlife* (London: Routledge, 2002).

15. The evolution of religious philosophy among the Jews, Christians, and Muslims from Philo to Spinoza constituted the backbone of Harry Austryn Wolfson's research.

16. Jan Assmann, *Moses the Egyptian: The Memory of Egypt in Western Monotheism* (Cambridge, MA: Harvard University Press, 1997).

of true sacrifice, to Augustine's famous *"Noli foras ire, in te ipsum redi; in interiore homine habitat veritas"* (Do not go outward; return within yourself. In the inward man dwells truth).[17] *Verus Israel*: the locution implies the discovery of the deep meaning of Scripture, under the surface, that only the Jews see. Similarly, true sacrifice refers to the sacrifice of Christian liturgy, where blood is not spilled. Augustine, on his side, proposed finding God within oneself; the movement of elevation and that of interiorization are identified with each other.[18] One might argue that a similar pattern of thought can be observed in Plotinus. No doubt we may speak of continuity between Greco-Roman and Christian conceptions of the self, as does, for instance, the British philosopher Richard Sorabji.[19] The essential difference, though, is that neither in Plotinus nor in Porphyry is such a requirement identified as essential to the religion of the collectivity. Therefore it seems to me that one may discern, alongside evident continuities, deep ruptures in the conception of the self. The requirement of truth at the very heart of religion is, in other words, the idea of faith. Paul Veyne has shown how the Greeks could not really believe in their myths.[20] But the Christians did believe in their myths and did adhere to them totally: *"Alithos anesti"* (Truly he is risen), according to the ritual words of the Easter liturgy.

My thesis, therefore, will be that the transformations of anthropological conceptions that we may detect in Late Antiquity

17. Augustine *De vera religione* 39.72. See also Charles Taylor, *Sources of the Self: The Making of the Modern Identity* (Cambridge, MA: Harvard University Press, 1989), 127–42.

18. See, for example, Philip Cary, *Augustine's Invention of the Inner Self: The Legacy of a Christian Platonist* (Oxford: Oxford University Press, 2000).

19. Richard Sorabji, "Soul and Self in Ancient Philosophy," in *From Soul to Self*, ed. M. James C. Crabbe (London: Routledge, 1999), 8–32. See also Henry Chadwick, "Philosophical Tradition and the Self," in *Late Antiquity: A Guide to the Postclassical World*, ed. Glen W. Bowersock, Peter Brown, and Oleg Grabar (Cambridge, MA: Harvard University Press, 1999), 60–81.

20. Paul Veyne, *Les Grecs ont-ils cru à leur mythes? Essai sur l'imagination constituante* (Paris: Seuil, 1983). Translated into English by Paula Wissing as *Did the Greeks Believe in Their Myths? An Essay on the Constitutive Imagination* (Chicago: University of Chicago Press, 1988).

are above all of a religious nature, and hence that their study is essential to a better comprehension of the religious transformations under the Roman Empire. Foucault, in his last years, devoted his efforts to the shift from the Greco-Roman care of the self (*epimeleia heautou*) to the Christian conception of the person, which he identified a little hastily with the denial of the body, resting his analysis on an overly limited corpus of texts. He had discerned, with great flair, some of the profound differences between the two phenomena, but he did not have the leisure to analyze them. Even if more time had been granted to him, though, I believe he would not have been able to succeed better in this task than Budé and many others before him, because he conceived of it, as they did, as a shift from ancient thought to Christian thought, thereby forgetting, or relegating to the background, the Jewish nature of the great Christian concepts. Without this Jewish dimension, it remains impossible to explain the great transformation of anthropological concepts of Late Antiquity. To give only one example, I will refer to the rather long description that Foucault gives of Philo's Therapeutes in *The Hermeneutics of the Subject*. Here Foucault gives his reader (previously, his listener) no indication of the Jewish identity of these Therapeutes, nor, a fortiori, of their spiritual proximity to the Essenes, hence to milieus close to the Jesus movement.[21] To read him, one might think that they were participants in a mystery cult.

The victory of Christianity in the Roman Empire cannot be truly understood as an *internal* transformation of Greco-Roman culture. It is with Jewish weapons that Christianity conquered the Roman Empire. Any taxonomy must call upon what Max Weber termed *Idealtypen*, and hence it excessively simplifies a complex and moving reality, which it transfixes and radicalizes. Rather it is a matter of grasping the vectors of this reality in an era of multiple cultural encounters, and the profound transformations that

21. Foucault, *Hermeneutics of the Subject*, 326. On Foucault's impact on the study of ancient Christianity, see Averil Cameron, "Redrawing the Map: Early Christian Territory after Foucault," *Journal of Roman Studies* 76 (1986): 266–71.

these encounters entail. The passage from pagan Rome to Christian Rome cannot be understood as a simple internal cultural mutation, a sort of parthenogenesis. A system of binary oppositions will not be convincing, either. The dichotomy Athens/Rome remains as insufficient as Athens/Jerusalem. To speak of an opposition between reason and force, or reason and faith, means going back to the perception of cultural conflicts rather than to their explanation. At the very least we are dealing with a triangle between Jerusalem, Athens, and Rome, and all the cultural combinations that flow from this. Since Tertullian's lapidary phrase "What is there in common between Athens and Jerusalem?"[22] people readily speak of the conflict between Athens and Jerusalem, between one attitude founded essentially on the values of reason and another that finds its inspiration in faith, in order to describe the passage from pagan Rome to Christian Rome. What people often forget, perhaps paradoxically, are the Jewish dimensions of this new Jerusalem, the Christian faith. The Christianization of the subject in the Roman Empire cannot be understood without an awareness of these dimensions. Neither imperial religion nor mystery cults could conceive of the transformation of interior life and of rational discipline. Such a transformation was only conceivable among the philosophers and among the Jews—in very different ways in each case, of course.

A tense relation exists between two archetypal conceptions of perfection that André-Jean Festugière contrasted long ago.[23] One of them insists on the similarity of nature between the soul and the divine world (discerning a kinship, or *sungeneia*, between the soul and the divine), while the other insists on the insurmountable distance between the two. The former, which is of Platonic origin (or at least was perceived as such by intellectuals in the Roman Empire), obviously is found above all among Hellenic writers, whereas the latter, founded on the biblical idea of *creatio*

---

22. "Quid ergo Athenae et Hierosolymae?" Tertullian *De Praescriptione haereticorum* 7.9.12.

23. André-Jean Festugière, *Le sage et le saint* (Paris: Cerf, 1974).

ex nihilo, is principally the privilege of Christian thinkers.[24] But things are obviously not so simple, and the depth of the Platonic influences (often very Stoicized) on the thought of patristic authors is such that these contrasting ideas are sometimes found in the same author. The former will lead to salvation through knowledge or the gnosis, a salvation depending on the transformation of the subject by its divinization, or *theiōsis*, through revelation and the realization of its profound nature. The second path leads to sanctity through *praxis* rather than through *theōria*. For the saint, it is a matter of transforming himself, changing (by a constant, almost superhuman, effort) his nature, which is defined as guilty because it participates in original sin; he tries to identify himself with Jesus Christ, the man-God. This *imitatio Christi* will become the very sign of the martyr, then of the monk.[25] The tension between these two poles is not only a reflection of the tension between pagan texts and Christian texts. The ideal of perfection reflected by the Gnostic texts represents, as has often been repeated since Adolf von Harnack, *die akute Hellenisierung des Christentums* (the radical Hellenization of Christianity). But this idea is also found among certain "orthodox" Christian thinkers, especially among those who were strongly influenced by Platonic currents.

I am thinking in particular of Clement of Alexandria, who before the end of the second century developed the model of a Christian gnosis at the confluence of Platonism and Stoicism. This gnosis ensures the salvation of the Christian sage, a salvation that cannot be totally independent of that of other people, less knowledgeable perhaps, but just as believing. For Clement, at the intersection of so-called Gnostic traditions, *gnōsis* (knowledge) can only be acquired after *pistis* (faith), as a result of con-

24. See Édouard Des Places, *Syngeneia: La parenté de l'homme avec Dieu, d'Homère à la patristique* (Paris: C. Klincksieck, 1964); and Pierre Courcelle, *Connais-toi toi-même, de Socrate à Saint Bernard*, 3 vols. (Paris: Études augustiniennes, 1974–75).

25. See, for example, Guy G. Stroumsa, *Savoir et salut* (Paris: Cerf, 1992), 145–62.

stant spiritual exercises, of a permanent *askēsis* (ascesis).[26] One might compare what Clement says in the *Stromateis* with the way in which Athanasius presents the ideal of life incarnated by Saint Antony in the desert. The tension between two modes of reflection on the self—one more conservative and concerned especially with cultivating the self; the other more dynamic, aiming at transforming it—is therefore not only a tension between Christian texts and "pagan" texts. It is found among philosophers as well as among Christians. In every case, there is a care of the self, which is expressed differently in each.

Michel Foucault, in his effort to find transformations of the care of the self in ancient thought, passed, almost without noticing it, from Plato's dialogues (in particular *Alcibiades I*) to the texts of the Roman Stoics, Seneca and Marcus Aurelius. Doing so, it seems to me he paid too little attention to middle Platonist and Neoplatonist (as well as to the neo-Pythagorean) traditions, which must have had a strong influence on the Christian intellectual tradition. The letters from Seneca to Lucilius, or the treatises of Plutarch (an eclectic writer, to be sure, but situating himself above all in the wake of middle Platonism), might be contrasted with certain writings of the third century: for example, Porphyry's *Letter to Marcella* or his passionate and instructive *On Abstinence*, or else the famous *Life of Apollonius of Tyana* by Philostratus of Athens. One finds reflected in such texts the idea that the human ideal requires one to surpass oneself and to be transformed from mortal into immortal, into a divine man (*theios anēr*).[27]

People have long wanted to find in biographies of Pythagoras, one by Porphyry and then one by Iamblichus, the very model of Christian hagiography, particularly in the first one (by date and in importance), the *Life of Antony* by Athanasius of Alex-

26. See, for example, Salvatore R. C. Lilla, *Clement of Alexandria: A Study in Christian Platonism and Gnosticism* (Oxford: Oxford University Press, 1971).

27. On this concept and its pertinence, see Carl H. Holladay, *Theios Aner in Hellenistic Judaism: A Critique of the Use of This Category in New Testament Christology* (Missoula, MT: Scholars Press, 1977).

andria. Thus Richard Reitzenstein, eminent representative of the *religionsgeschichtliche Schule* (the movement called "School of the History of Religions"), compared the literary forms of hagiography, but without speculating about the specific differences between the two cases.[28] That numerous characteristics of the philosopher as *theios anēr* are also those of the *gerōn*, the Christian saintly old man, is certainly not in doubt. But one would like a more detailed analysis of the specificity of each. Can one be specific about the origin of the differences between pagan and Christian hagiographies? This origin, it seems to me, lies in the idea of moral, rather than intellectual, progress, which is the supreme requirement of the Christian spiritual guide.

The idea of transformation of the internal life remained unknown to the official religion of the ancient city, as well as to mystery cults. But since the Hellenistic period, in the urban culture of the Mediterranean basin and the Near East, one could move from one religious belief to another, from one cultic practice to another. In other words, the idea of conversion was born and was applied just as much to philosophical schools as to religious sects, as we know from Arthur Darby Nock's classic study.[29] The philosophers formed sects, "heresies" (thus Josephus, describing the Pharisees, Sadducees, and Essenes). Later, it would be the Christians' turn to identify themselves as "schools" of thought, like philosophers, so as to receive a certain legitimacy—not forgetting that they conceived of themselves as belonging to a school that was essentially different from others, since its philosophy remained "barbarian" but was clearly differentiated from the Greek philosophical schools.[30]

28. For a succinct presentation of these problems, see the introduction by G. J. M. Bartelink to his edition of *La Vie d'Antoine*, Sources chrétiennes, no. 400 (Paris: Cerf, 1994).

29. Arthur Darby Nock, *Conversion: The Old and the New in Religion from Alexander the Great to Augustine of Hippo* (Oxford: Oxford University Press, 1933).

30. See, for example, Robert L. Wilken, "Alexandria: A School of Training in Virtue," in *Schools of Thought in the Christian Tradition*, ed. Patrick Henry (Philadelphia: Fortress Press, 1984), 15–30.

But philosophical conversion was not the same as Christian conversion. The former was defined as *epistrophē*, as returning. Someone who converted to philosophy—that is to say, someone who joined a philosophical school—had to accept its rules of living, which were sometimes very rigid, especially for neophytes (those who were newly integrated into a Pythagorean community were required, as at Qumran, to keep silent for five years!).[31] He had to turn away from the world, from his previous way of life, in order to care only for himself, for the purification of his deeper self, that is to say, of his intellect, so as to succeed in rediscovering and in expressing his divine essence.

Christian conversion, by contrast, is above all *metanoia*, repenting. Of course, this is a Jewish idea, since one finds it at the source of Christianity with John the Baptist. Conversion to Christianity implied, as did *epistrophē*, a return, but this return was much more moral than intellectual. The turning toward God was foremost a return to oneself, an attempt to understand the nature of sins that had effaced (or at the very least obscured) the image of God that man was supposed to represent.[32] The distance between the two conversions is not just between the small part of the divine represented by the *nous* (spirit) and the image of the divine that is man—often as a whole, body as well as soul—among the first Christian thinkers. This distance also reflects major anthropological differences. Each has a fundamentally different conception of the human person. These differences are anchored in the very nature of Christianity, that is to say, in a religious attitude.

The Hellenization of forms of Christian thought in Late Antiquity (especially in apologetic literature) blunted some of these differences by effecting a play of equivalences—a gambit already known in Jewish Hellenistic apologetics. For example, the idea

31. See Justin Taylor, *Pythagoreans and Essenes: Structural Parallels* (Paris: Peeters, 2004).

32. See Annick Charles-Saget, ed., *Retour, repentir et constitution du soi* (Paris: J. Vrin, 1998).

of the resurrection of the body, which Christianity had received from Judaism, was particularly repugnant to Greco-Roman intellectuals. Although Christians could certainly not abandon a central tenet of their faith, some Christian thinkers, under Platonic influence, tended to identify the resurrection of body with the immortality of the soul, although these are two radically different conceptions.

Another central conception of Christianity, divine incarnation, also revolted philosophers. The gods might take human forms, of course, but why one single incarnation in the history of humanity and, more precisely, why in a crucified body? The Christian refuses the idea of death, revolts against it, even when he pursues it in martyrdom. After Paul, the idea of the sacrifice of the Son of God does not seem tolerable (even in a pattern of thought that cultivates paradox) except through the assurance of his resurrection.

In contrast to the Christian thinker, the Greco-Roman sage, either Stoic or Platonic, wants to learn to accept death. For him, it is neither a matter of accepting the laws of nature nor of revolting against them. For Plutarch—who is, let us not forget, both a priest of Apollo and a Greek-speaking Roman intellectual—the sage is someone who knows how to recognize his limits and consequently to live without *hubris* (excess), so as to succeed in integrating with nature. In his *Peri Euthumias* (*On Inner Serenity*), Plutarch involves his friend Paccius in spiritual exercises. The unhappiness of men comes from their being distant from nature. Asceticism here aims at recovering lost happiness, of which *autarkeia* (autarky) is the first condition. Happiness, in effect, resides in the tranquillity that we may find beyond our own strength. Not forcing one's nature is what allows one to reach the refuge of peace and indifference to the world, and in particular to others. To try to discern these transformations of the self under the Roman Empire, we might examine certain models of the ideal person that are found in the literatures of the first centuries. The care of the self is, by definition, reserved for the elites; but Christianity proposes (and to a large extent will succeed in) imposing its new model of the elite, one founded on a religious practice that is supererogatory and often eccentric or ostentatious, by those whom Max Weber called "religious virtuosos."

We are very far from the interior life in Augustine, for whom divine truth is not peace, refuge, and indifference, but rather the total demand of the relation to the Other, in an indelible tension. The implications of this difference are at once metaphysical, moral, and political.

Under the empire, the ideal of the sage is therefore different from that of the Greek philosopher. Above all, it is no longer a matter of his possessing a certain exclusive knowledge (even if it is a negative knowledge: "I know that I know nothing") that renders him superior to other men or makes him a more accomplished man. It is supremely a matter of behavior, of an attitude of constancy and acceptance in the face of a reality that is both unchangeable and insignificant.[33]

For the Jews of the period of the Second Temple, the model man was usually neither the sage nor the saint, but in traditional fashion the prophet. In direct contrast to the sage, the prophet does not resign himself. His identity is the struggle, often quixotic, against power, in particular against spiritual power—an oxymoron and thus by definition illegitimate. In the Hellenistic world, the Jews had discovered the value of the eminently Greek idea of *paideia*. In applying it to the study of their own cultural tradition, their Law, they later, in the rabbinic period, made it the central value of their cultural identity: *Talmud Torah ke-neged kulam* (the study of the Torah is as important as all the other divine commandments combined). It has recently been shown that in rabbinic Judaism, the study of the Law represented a central value of Late Antiquity.[34]

Above everything else that the Christians inherited from the

33. See Pierre Hadot, "La figure du sage dans l'Antiquité gréco-latine," in *Études de philosophie ancienne* (Paris: Les Belles Lettres, 1998), 232–57.

34. Michael L. Satlow, "And on the Earth You Shall Sleep: *Talmud Torah* and Rabbinic Asceticism," *Journal of Religion* (2003): 204–25.

Jews was the ideal of the prophet. In a sense, their messiah had been the perfect prophet. In early Christianity, as in the first stage of Islam, before charisma was routinized (to use, again, a Weberian term), the prophets were still active. Thus, at the start of the second century, the *Didache* mentions them alongside apostles, teachers, bishops, and deacons. Yet the Montanists, who cultivated active prophecy toward the end of the same century, were quickly considered to be heretics.[35] The figure of the prophet was thus transformed into that of the saint. In the Christian communities of Late Antiquity, the saint (the holy man so well studied by Peter Brown) played a role comparable to that of the prophet: the axis of the community, at once central and marginal.[36] The saint confronts the bishop: it is once again the conflict between the prophet and the priest that is played out, but under different conditions and with new stakes.

Thus in the first centuries of the Roman Empire, one finds a series of *Idealtypen*: the sage, the Gnostic, and the saint. It is not excessively simplistic to note that among the "pagans," the sage and the Gnostic, in particular, were in competition with each other. Meanwhile, among the Christians, the most noticeable polarity was between the Gnostic and the saint. Among the Jews, finally, it seems to me that the principal tension was the one between the sage and the saint (the latter, like the priest, went into decline after the destruction of the Temple: "*ḥakham ʿadif mi-navi*" [the sage is superior to the prophet], according to a Tal-

35. See Christine Trevett, *Montanism: Gender, Authority, and the New Prophecy* (Cambridge: Cambridge University Press, 1996). On the prophets of the first stages of Islam, see Yohanan Friedmann, "Finality of Prophethood in Sunni Islam," *Jerusalem Studies in Arabic and Islam* 7 (1986): 177–215.

36. Peter Brown's seminal article "The Rise and Function of the Holy Man in Late Antiquity," published first in the *Journal of Roman Studies* 61 (1971): 80–101, gave rise to a new sensitivity to the religious history of Late Antiquity. See, for example, the appreciation by Averil Cameron, "On Defining the Holy Man," in *The Cult of Saints in Late Antiquity and the Middle Ages: Essays on the Contribution of Peter Brown*, ed. James Howard-Johnston and Paul A. Hayward (Oxford: Oxford University Press, 1999), 27–34; see also Lellia Cracco Ruggini, "All'ombra di Momigliano: Peter Brown e la mutazione del Tardoantico," *Rivista Storica Italiana* 100 (1988): 739–67.

mudic adage).[37] In each of these cases, there is a tension between two attitudes on the part of elites, one more intellectual, the other more "spiritual"—or more charismatic and soteriological.

Both the sage and the Gnostic represent transformations of Greek philosophy. The *epistēmē* (knowledge) is turned into either a *gnōsis*, a soteriological knowledge, or into a *phronēsis*, a way of being, more than a system of thought. The saint, the emblematic figure of Late Antiquity, represents a transformation of the Jewish prophet. Prophecy is obviously not particular to the Jews. We find prophets in various societies of the Near East and in the Mediterranean world in Greece, for instance. The specificity of Hebrew prophecy lies in the central place it gives to the ethical requirement. With the prophet, then the saint, ethical concern becomes an integral part of religion. "Be holy, as I am holy." Therefore the ideal of sanctity represents the care of the self, but also more than a care for the self alone, for the ethics of the self passes by way of the other. Roughly speaking, let us say that the individual cannot in this context save himself alone. Here we detect a striking difference from the idea of the sage as found, for example, in Seneca or Plutarch.[38] In each of the cultural milieus that we are dealing with here, the tensions between the poles are of a dialectical nature. In particular, this means that the nature of the pagan sage will not be the same as that of the Jewish sage: the former stands in relation to the Gnostic (for example, think of the authors and readers of Hermetic texts), and the latter in relation to the saint. So the Jewish sage will be influenced by the ideal of sanctity, and Jewish wisdom will take more account of the other, his salvation and his education, than does Greco-Roman wisdom. Inversely, among Jewish saints, in tension as they are with the sages, the intellectual side will be expressed in a different way than among Christian saints, who stand in dialectical opposition to the Gnostics. Similarly, Chris-

---

37. Babylonian Talmud, *Baba Batra* 12a.

38. On the figure of the sage and his religiosity in Seneca, see the admirable preface by Paul Veyne to Sénèque, *Entretiens, Lettres à Lucilius* (Paris: R. Laffont, 1993).

tian *gnosis* will reflect an interest in the ethical (and hence ascetic or encratic) dimension of salvation that is often hard to find in pagan Gnostic texts.

Thus ethics and the care for the other are in Christianity an integral part of the religious sensibility. Women, non-citizens, and slaves find for the first time a significant role in religion. This does not mean that Christian ethical rigor must be contrasted with a pagan moral laxity, but that the ethical was not for the pagans an integral part of religion as it was for the Christians or for the Jews.[39]

Other aspects are no less essential. For the sage or the pagan Gnostic, the self is to be constructed or sculpted, to use the expression of Plotinus (*Enneads* 1.6.9.13). For the Jewish sage or saint, for the Christian Gnostic or saint, the self was above all to be decoded and conquered. An "exegesis of the soul" had to be offered.[40] For the Irish monk Columba around the middle of the sixth century, it was by making no headway in the world that one might hope to conquer oneself.[41] To conquer oneself, to master oneself—not, as Foucault used to say, to deny oneself.

Interest in the self's past and in its present is essential. Wondering about one's sins, understanding their nature, is a central aspect of the therapeutic process of the self, open in principle to every man and woman, which permits his or her purification (ethical rather than ritual), a necessary requirement for repentance, hence for salvation. Thus Theodoret of Cyprus, a theologian of monasticism in the fifth century, wrote a book dealing with the "therapeutics of Hellenic maladies." It is in this sense

39. On the role of ethics in ancient Christianity, see Wayne A. Meeks, *The Moral World of the First Christians* (Philadelphia: Fortress Press, 1986), and Jan L. Womer, *Morality and Ethics in Early Christianity* (Philadelphia: Fortress Press, 1987). See also Jean-Michel Carrié and Aline Rousselle, *L'Empire romain en mutation: Des Sévères à Constantin 192–337* (Paris: Seuil, 1999), 314, stressing the transformation of relations between ethics and religion with the advent of Christianity.

40. See *Nag Hammadi Codex* 2.6.

41. Columba *Sermon* 3.3. I cite the translation of Arthur G. Holder in *Religions of Late Antiquity in Practice*, ed. Richard Valantasis (Princeton, NJ: Princeton University Press, 2000), 109–21.

that Adolf von Harnack, with Nietzschean tones, would speak of Christianity as a religion for the sick.[42]

The return to the self (*teshuva* in Hebrew signifies the return to God, of course, but also the return to the self) requires an intense interest in the sinning self, a reading, or a hermeneutic of the self. Such an attitude implies an enlargement of the self, which includes diverse aspects of the personality considered by pagan thinkers to be unworthy of interest. See, for example, the essential difference between Marcus Aurelius's *Meditations* and Augustine's *Confessions*. It is the latter writer's profound psychological interest in the sinning self that gives the *Confessions* their modern tone and that makes it the first authentic autobiography, as Georg Misch remarked a long time ago. Misch added, in speaking of the *Confessions*, that it launched one of the more profound changes in the European unveiling of the self.[43] Here we can discern the appearance of a new sensibility. Before him, nobody (not even a poet) had been capable of speaking of himself. Paul Veyne notes that "nothing is more misleading than the use of 'I' in Greco-Roman poetry."[44] Of course, Augustine was an unequaled psychological genius, but in the East we also find Evagrius Ponticus, a magisterial analyst of the weaknesses of the soul among the "ultra-perfectionists" of the monastic desert.

This idea of a self to be decoded, to be recognized, to be read, is not in fact independent of the idea (to be treated in a following chapter) of a religion of the Book. Religion, including religious worship, is above all the meditation on texts, with a central place granted to texts dealing with the individual, with the individual

42. Adolf von Harnack, *The Mission and Expansion of Christianity in the First Three Centuries* (1902; repr., New York: G. P. Putman's, 1904–5), 109. See also Antigone Samellas, *Death in the Eastern Mediterranean (50–600 A.D.): The Christianization of the East: An Interpretation* (Tübingen: Mohr Siebeck, 2002), 45, where the author explains how Christianity proposed a psychotherapeutic ethic accessible to everyone.

43. Georg Misch, *A History of Autobiography in Antiquity*, 2 vols. (1907; repr., Cambridge, MA: Harvard University Press, 1951), 1:17.

44. In his chapter on the Roman Empire, in Paul Veyne, ed., *Histoire de la vie privée*, vol. 1. I quote from the English edition, *A History of Private Life*, vol. 1, *From Pagan Rome to Byzantium* (Cambridge, MA: Harvard University Press, 1987), 231.

sinner, in particular the Psalms, a meditation that the Christians learned from Second Temple Judaism.[45]

With the Christianization of the Roman Empire, the principal transformation of the care of the self is due principally to a broadening of the concept of the human person. Christianity, this "*akute Hellenisierung und Romanisierung des Judentums*" (this radical Hellenization and Romanization of Judaism), as we might say by paraphrasing Harnack, bursts the limits of the person as it was known in Greek and Roman thought. If sin takes a central place, this is because, for Christian authors, the definition of the person includes the body as much as the intellect. It is not only a matter of knowing if the soul is or is not corporeal. As we know, various Greek conceptions of the soul did consider it as corporeal. It is now a matter of the body itself, which constitutes an integral part of the person, since it is created by God in his image (it is only Platonic Christian thinkers who would see the *imago Dei* in the soul alone). The body will be resurrected at the end of time, just as Jesus Christ, Son of God incarnated in a human body, was resurrected in this body after his death. Still more than for the Jews, then, the centrality of the physical body in the definition of the person assumes among Christians a preponderant and essential place. Jesus Christ died in the body in order for us to be saved from death through the resurrection of the body. *Caro salutis cardo:* the flesh is the axis of salvation, according to Tertullian's pregnant formulation. Both funerary inscriptions and church mosaics reveal the importance of this resurrection in Late Antiquity—for example, in the numerous citations of verses from Corinthians 1:15 that deal with the resurrected body.

The two Jewish conceptions of *creatio ex nihilo* and *homo imago Dei* had permitted the recognition of the body as an integral part of the human person: it is man as a whole who is

45. See the fine analyses by Brian Stock, *Augustine the Reader: Meditation, Self-Knowledge, and the Ethics of Interpretation* (Cambridge, MA: Harvard University Press, 1996). See also, by the same author, *After Augustine: The Meditative Reader and the Text* (Philadelphia: University of Pennsylvania Press, 2001), in particular chapter 1, "Reading and Self-Knowledge."

created, like the material world, by a good and just God, and he is made in the image of his creator. The resurrection of the body at the end of time would seal this integration of body and soul. The idea of divine incarnation, and of his Son's resurrection as the promise of our own, could only strengthen this perception of the value of the body. The dualism composed of the deep Platonic influences on many Christian intellectuals and the no less deep tendencies to reject the body in encratic asceticism would no doubt blur the earliest Christian anthropology; but it will not succeed in erasing it.[46]

Repenting, through reading the soul as much as reading the Psalms, is therefore a prime point in the work on oneself that the Christian—in particular, the ascetic—must achieve. This repenting implies a whole system of public penitence, visible by the community that sets the conditions by which it agrees to reintegrate the sinner. We see to what point knowledge has changed meaning: it is now a public recognition of sin and a no less public expression of repentance, an announcement before the community of the price to be paid. In the system of *paenitentia secunda*, developed starting in Late Antiquity and perfected in the West during the High Middle Ages, we have the concrete representation of the Christian consciousness of the dimensions of the personality and the way in which care of the individual self is integrated into the care that the collectivity takes of itself.[47]

Michel Foucault has proposed seeing in the Christian attitude toward the self (by referring especially to the writings of John Cassian, hence to Eastern monasticism as it was propagated in the West) a will to suppress the self, to annihilate it, or at least to integrate it within a much larger framework. In a sense, but only in a sense, Foucault was right. He saw that the accent placed on the human person as an independent monad, alone re-

46. See Stroumsa, *Savoir et salut*, 199–223. See also Judith Perkins, *The Suffering Self: Pain and Narrative Representation in the Early Christian Era* (London: Routledge, 1995).

47. Developed in Stroumsa, *Barbarian Philosophy*, 158–68.

sponsible—and responsible only—for care of itself, is not found among Christians. But his insistence on the limitation, even the suppression, of the self among Christian thinkers of Late Antiquity leads us along a false path. For it is not a *limitation* but indeed an *enlargement* of the person that the Christian thinkers achieve. They accomplish this by anchoring themselves in the very bases of their religion. The transformation of the person observed with Christianity therefore enlarges the limits of the self rather than narrowing them. The Christian self does not disappear into the community; it becomes, on the contrary, emblematic. The philosopher naturally possessed, through his intellect, a *sungeneia* (kinship) with the divine. But this *sungeneia* came at the cost of the exclusion of the body from his deep self. The Christian, if he does not possess such divinity within himself, no less strives to approach as much as possible the divine Savior by his constant imitation, thanks to his efforts and his asceticism.[48]

It seems to me that the highly ambiguous status of the reflexivity developed by Christian thinkers is what misled Foucault. As we have seen, the ambiguous status is in fact due to the disappearance of the *sungeneia* between the human and the divine world. The incommensurability between the world of creatures and the Creator prevents a narcissism of the self: to turn to the self is above all, now, to re-form oneself. And the Jewish or Christian reforming of the self is above all a moral reform, starting with the recognition of sins and repentance. The great caesura in the self is no longer between body and soul, but between the sinning self and the saved self. The path of reform, moreover, is no longer reserved for intellectual elites, but is open to every man and every woman, and open to love of the other, by which the love of God now passes.[49] The new care of the self cannot ignore ethics and intersubjectivity. The most extreme of the heroes of exhibitionist

---

48. Developed in Stroumsa, *Savoir et salut*, 199–223.

49. If here one discerns echoes of Emmanuel Lévinas, this is not by chance. It is with him, more than forty years ago, that I read for the first time Plato, the Talmud, and Teresa of Avila.

asceticism is no doubt the holy *salos*, the fool in Christ, promised a long future, from the monastic desert to Dostoyevsky's Prince Mishkin. This limit-case character, making like a beast to play an angel and toying with the world (*empaizein tōi kosmōi*), also ends up returning to this world he had fled. Even *he* does not succeed in saving himself all alone.[50]

The new discourse on dreams found in patristic literature also reflects the new status of the self among Christians. With the victory of Christianity, the interpreters of dreams, who had been well-known in Antiquity, disappear. The dream less announces the future than reveals to conscience its culpability, calling it to penitence. I tried a long time ago to show that the Church fathers, in rejecting Gnosis, were given to a "disenchantment with the world" (*Entzauberung der Welt*), which Max Weber did not see appearing until the Protestant Reformation. It is thanks to their new conception of religious life, integrating thought and ethics, that the fathers were able to vanquish the Gnostic temptation.[51] The Christianized dream, too, reflects such a "disenchantment" by expressing the individual and by sending him back into himself, rather than by reflecting external realities. Artemidorus was interested in dreams as the key to the future. The revolution established by Freudian introspection finds its sources in the Christian thought and practice of Late Antiquity. If Gustav von Grunebaum was right to say that we no longer have need of a *Wahrtraum* (a true dream), it is to the anthropological revolution of ancient Christianity that we owe this.[52]

"It was the Christians who made the moral person a metaphysical entity once they realized its religious power. Our own notion of the human person is still basically the Christian notion." Thus Marcel Mauss wrote it in his seminal article of 1938, "A Category of the Human Mind: The Notion of Person, the

50. There is an analysis of Saint Simeon Salos in Stroumsa, *Barbarian Philosophy*, 228–43.

51. See Stroumsa, *Savoir et salut*, 163–81.

52. Stroumsa, *Barbarian Philosophy*, 204–22.

Notion of 'Self.'" Mauss concludes his very short chapter on the Christian person: "He [Cassiodorus] failed to make of this individual substance what it now is, a consciousness and a category."[53] I hope that the preceding pages will at least have indicated, even if they were not able to demonstrate it, that the new care of the self that develops in Late Antiquity, especially thanks to Christian thinkers and the virtuosos of asceticism, was also a conscience, moral as much as intellectual.

53. Marcel Mauss, "A Category of the Human Mind: The Notion of Person, the Notion of 'Self,'" in *Sociology and Psychology: Essays*, trans. Ben Brewster (London: Routledge and Kegan Paul, 1979), 85–86.

2

The Rise of Religions of the Book

In his *Treatise on Principles* (4.2.4), one of the great intellectual monuments of ancient Christianity, Origen of Caesarea represents the sacred text as tripartite, composed like a human being of a body, a soul, and a mind. Thus every individual can understand divine Scripture at the level that suits him. The Jews, who knew divine writings that had formerly been revealed to them only in their corporeal (that is to say, literal) aspect, developed (instead of the legitimate interpretation of Christians) a hermeneutic within which circulated a whole series of absurd interpretations without any true relation with the text. Origen is manifestly alluding here to juridical commentaries, *midrashei halakhah*, which he could hear in the voice of the rabbis with whom he debated at Caesarea (*Peri Archōn* 4.3.2).[1] His remark indeed reflects

---

1. On Origen's biblical hermeneutic, see Henri de Lubac, *Histoire et esprit: L'intelligence de l'Écriture d'après Origène* (1950; repr., Paris: Aubier, 2002), which remains a classic. On contacts between Origen and the rabbis, see Nicholas R. M. de Lange, *Origen and the Jews: Studies in Jewish-Christian Relations in Third-Century Palestine* (Cambridge: Cambridge University Press, 1976). I have studied an aspect of these relations in *Hidden Wisdom: Esoteric Traditions and the Roots of Christian Mysticism*, Studies in the History of Religions, no. 70 (1996; repr., Leiden: Brill, 2005), 109–31.

the great difference in attitude toward the sacred text between Jews and Christians at the time, one of the differences I would like to reflect upon in this chapter.

We saw above how there developed in the Roman Empire the idea of a reflexive self, to be read like a book. The reading or the chanting of Psalms, as has been mentioned, represents in this framework a perfect path for the reading of the self, of a sinning self, and hence for the definition of identity.[2] Under the empire, different changes in the status and technique of writing and of reading, such as the appearance of the codex and a new status of the scribe (to which we will return), allowed the slow development of silent reading, which in its turn encouraged a dialectic between reading the Book and reading the self.[3] The interiorization of reading represents an essential aspect of the transformation of culture, of course, but also, in a more precise way, of religion under the Roman Empire—an aspect that has not been sufficiently stressed. Among the Christians, the law of God was read also to understand *oneself* and to re-form *oneself*.[4] Of

2. This is particularly important among monastic communities. See James W. McKinnon, "Desert Monasticism and the Later Fourth-Century Psalmodic Movement," *Music and Letters* 75 (1994): 505–21; as well as Peter Jeffery, "Monastic Reading and the Emerging Roman Chant Repertory," in *Western Plainchant in the First Millennium: Studies in the Medieval Liturgy and Its Music*, ed. Sean Gallager et al. (Aldershot, UK: Ashgate, 2003), 45–103. I am indebted to Christopher Page for calling my attention to this important essay. Jeffery argues that the "personal" way of reading the Psalms, applying them to oneself as if looking in a mirror (59), dates from the fourth century and is essentially monastic.

3. See, for example, Guglielmo Cavallo, "Du *volumen* au *codex*: La lecture dans le monde romain," in *Histoire de la lecture dans le monde occidental*, ed. Guglielmo Cavallo and Roger Chartier (Paris: Seuil, 2001), 85–114. Cavallo has contributed more than anybody to our understanding of the revolution in the history of the book with the shift from the scroll to the volume. See Emmanuelle Valette-Cagnac, *La lecture à Rome: Rites et pratiques* (Paris: Belin, 1997). See also Catherine Salles, *Lire à Rome* (Paris: Les Belles Lettres, 1992).

4. On the private reading of the Bible among the Christians of the first centuries, see Adolf von Harnack, *Über den privaten Gebrauch der heiligen Schriften in der alten Kirche*, Beiträge zur Einleitung in das Neue Testament, no. 5 (Leipzig: Hinrich, 1912). See also Guglielmo Cavallo, "Lire, écrire et mémoriser les Saintes Écritures," in *Des Alexandries*, ed. Christian Jacob (Paris: Bibliothèque nationale de France, 2003), 87–101.

all Christian texts, those that describe the life, death, and resurrection of Jesus Christ are by far the more important. For the Christian, it is not only a matter, above all, of knowing what Jesus did (or said), but indeed of trying to imitate him. The *imitatio Christi* soon becomes the requirement of a perfect Christian life, by martyrdom at first and then after the fourth century by ascetic living. Jesus is the *exemplum* par excellence.[5] And it is the sacred text, at its very heart, that gives us the life of Jesus, his words, his death, and his resurrection. A myth, then, of great simplicity— and most especially, a *single* myth that is identified with the text that carries it.

Later, as we shall see, even the Christian saint (in Byzantium, for example) is represented as a text, to be read and commented upon.[6] Here we perceive an essential difference from Greek mythology: here there is only a single story (let us leave aside for a moment the multiplicity of the Gospels), and in this story it is faith that defines Christian identity, as explained to us in the anonymous epistle to Diognetus before the end of the second century: the Christians have in common neither land nor language nor clothing—all things that ordinarily define collective identity (see chapter 4). Thus they have to be conceived of as a new sort of people, unknown until then: a people defined by their belief in a single myth, preserved in a sacred writing.

When treating the first centuries of the Roman Empire as a key period for observing the phenomenon that I propose to call "the rise of religions of the Book," it should certainly not be forgotten that some religious movements, for a long time already and in various civilizations, had developed around a sacred book

5. See Peter Brown, "The Saint as Exemplar in Late Antiquity," *Representations* 1 (1983): 1–25, in particular 10, "The Exemplar of All Exemplars."

6. Paul Magdalino, "'What We Heard in the Lives of the Saints We Have Seen with Our Own Eyes': The Holy Man as Literary Text in Tenth-Century Constantinople," in *The Cult of the Saints in Late Antiquity and the Early Middle Ages: Essays on the Contribution of Peter Brown*, ed. James Howard-Johnston and Paul A. Hayward (Oxford: Oxford University Press, 1999), 83–113.

or books and their authorized commentaries.[7] Here we may speak of synchronization. This is notably true of Orphism, Zoroastrianism, and Hinduism. Among the Jews since the first exile, the Torah had served as the "portable homeland," to use Heinrich Heine's expression. During the period of the Second Temple, Judaism saw the proliferation of numerous sects, each proposing a different interpretation of Scripture. The same era saw the redaction of a whole literature that has usually been called "apocryphal and pseudepigraphical literature of the Old Testament." The correlation between these two phenomena—the multiplication of writings and that of sects—is certainly not due to chance.[8] People still debate, sometimes passionately, the nature of the writings discovered at Qumran, on the shores of the Dead Sea, shortly after the end of the Second World War.[9] Whatever they may represent (either the library of an Essene settlement or else the depository for books brought from Jerusalem and representing all of

7. For a comparative study of the transformation of sacrificial religions into religions of the Book, see Barbara Holdrege, *Veda and Torah: Transcending the Textuality of Scripture* (Albany: State University of New York Press, 1996). See also Jan Assmann, *Die mosaische Unterscheidung; oder, Der Preis des Monotheismus* (Munich: Carl Hanser, 2003), 145–51, that proposes a phenomenological approach to "cultural religions" and "religions of the Book." On this last concept, see Bernhard Lang, "Buchreligion," in *Handbuch religionswissenschaftlicher Grundbegriffe*, ed. Hubert Cancik, Burkhard Gladigow, and Matthias Laubscher (Stuttgart: W. Kohlhammer, 1990), 2:143–65. See further Jan N. Bremmer, "From Holy Books to Holy Bible: An Itinerary from Ancient Greece to Modern Islam via Second Temple Judaism and Early Christianity," in *Authoritative Scriptures in Ancient Judaism*, ed. M. Popović (supplements to the *Journal of the Study of Judaism*; Leiden: Brill, forthcoming). On "holy books" in Greek religion, see Albert Henrichs, "*Hieroi logoi* and *hierai bibloi*: The (Unwritten) Margins of the Sacred in Ancient Greece," *Harvard Studies in Classical Philology* 101 (2003): 207–66.

8. See Albert Baumgarten, *The Flourishing of Jewish Sects in the Maccabean Era: An Interpretation* (Leiden: Brill, 1997). See further Frederick M. Denny and Rodney L. Taylor, eds., *The Holy Book in Comparative Perspective* (Columbia: University of South Carolina, 1985).

9. See Edna Ullmann-Margalit, *Out of the Cave: A Philosophical Inquiry into the Dead Sea Scrolls Research* (Cambridge, MA: Harvard University Press, 2006).

Jewish literature at the time), one should note the great number of writings found at Qumran.[10]

Thus the rise of Judaism as a religion of the Book precedes the birth of Christianity. What is still more remarkable, though, is the total disappearance (or almost so) of books in the culture of rabbinic Judaism, a disappearance that has not been enough taken into account and that remains still largely unexplained. The rise of Christianity may have something to do with this astonishing phenomenon: it seems in effect (the rarity of sources and the difficulties raised by their interpretation impose here the greatest caution) that Jews and Christians, in their efforts to distinguish themselves from each other, were forced to develop different practices of writing.[11] For the Christians, as for the Manichaeans, writing preserved the truth, which otherwise would be mixed with falsehood.[12] By contrast, the Jews composed a whole oral literature that they carefully avoided putting into writing. Their culture of commentary was oral to such an extent that the references to biblical verses in rabbinic literature are not introduced by the formula "thus it is written" but by "*she-ne'emar*" (as it is *said*). And this is not a unique case. The example of the Avesta's Gathas, the most ancient texts of the Zoroastrian tradition, shows that a sacred literature may be conserved with very great precision in solely oral fashion for even a millennium.[13] Rabbinic literature of the first Christian centuries and of Late

10. For an estimation of the number of scrolls at Qumran (901), see Daniel Stökl Ben Ezra, "Old Caves and Young Caves: A Statistical Reevaluation of a Qumran Consensus," in *Dead Sea Discoveries* 14 (2007): 317. See also Markus Bockmuehl, "Qumran Commentaries in Graeco-Roman Context," in *Text, Thought, and Practice in Qumran and Early Christianity*, ed. Daniel Schwartz and Ruth Clements (forthcoming).

11. See, for example, Birger Gerhardsson, *Memory and Manuscript: Oral Tradition and Written Transmission in Rabbinic Judaism and Early Christianity* (Uppsala: Gleerup, 1961).

12. To give one example among a thousand, see a text redacted in the beginning of the fifth century, the prologue of Marcus Diaconus, in his *Life of Porphyry, Bishop of Gaza*, ed. and trans. Henri Grégoire and M. A. Kugener (Paris: Les Belles Lettres, 1930).

13. See Shaul Shaked, "Scripture and Exegesis in Zoroastrianism," in *Homer, the Bible, and Beyond: Literary and Religious Canons in the Ancient World*, ed. Margalit

Antiquity—the Mishnah, the Beraitot, the two redactions of the Talmud (the Palestinian Talmud and the Babylonian Talmud), the first great collections of midrash (*midrash halakhah*, or ritual, as much as the *midrash haggadah*, or narrative)—is entirely an oral literature. The written redaction of multiple independent texts and then their compilation into the great collections came much later, without it being always possible to offer a precise dating.[14] I cannot enter here into a technical description of the many problems posed by these facts. I would only like to raise the hypothesis that it is the very recognition of the centrality of the Book in their religion that prevented the rabbis from writing. The Book of the Torah is for them so sacred that this sacredness reverberates in the very idea of a book: there is only *one* book, which was revealed by God, and there can never be another. Any commentary should be expressed in a medium other than writing, hence the idea of oral law alongside the written law.[15] One must add that the multiplicity of books reflects the variety of sectarian ideas condemned with the development of the idea of orthodoxy. Finally, the Christiano-Gnostic threat, founded as it was on all this apocryphal literature, strengthened among the rabbis the need for censorship of texts circulating alongside the Torah books on the way to canonization. Any phenomenon of canonization, indeed, bears the reverse process of censorship, and any cultural memory reflects a planned collective forgetting.[16]

With the destruction of the Temple and the end of sacrifices, the priests were marginalized. Various sects, moreover, such as the Sadducees and the Essenes, practically disappeared. The sages

---

Finkelberg and Guy G. Stroumsa, Jerusalem Studies in Religion and Culture, no. 2 (Leiden: Brill, 2003), 63–74.

14. See Günter Stemberger, *Introduction to the Talmud and Midrash* (Edinburgh: T. and T. Clark, 1996).

15. On this very complex problem, see, for example, Martin S. Jaffee, *Torah in the Mouth: Writing and Oral Tradition in Palestinian Judaism, 200 BCE–400 CE* (Oxford: Oxford University Press, 2001).

16. The relations between the phenomena of canonization and censorship have been well studied in Aleida Assmann and Jan Assmann, eds., *Kanon und Zensur: Archäologie der literarischen Kommunikation*, vol. 2 (Munich: Fink, 1987).

or rabbis who considered themselves as heirs of the Pharisees remained the only group to conserve a spiritual authority.[17] This does not mean of course that the sages did not have any enemies, any competitors for religious hegemony, such as the *minim* of rabbinic literature—a generic name identifying various competing currents, such as Jewish-Christians, dualists, and Gnostics of all stripes.[18] But the rabbis, unlike Christian heresiologists, tried to give the fewest details possible about the heretics that they were combating, preferring to "kill them by silence."

The extreme simplification of mythology—that is to say, of the fabulating function of religion—may be discerned in the Christian story. It is found again, *mutatis mutandis*, in the radical simplification of the idea of the book effected in rabbinic Judaism. Thus we may speak of the appearance of a "textual culture" in the Greco-Roman world only with the *grammatika*, meaning not before the third century of our era. At this time the traditional intertextual culture of the Jews itself passed from writing to orality.

Beyond the Jews and the Christians, one notices in the Near East of Late Antiquity, in the centuries running from Jesus to Muhammad (via Mani), a succession of religious movements founded on holy or revealed books. On this subject, Wilfred Cantwell Smith was able to speak of a "scriptural movement" in the Late Antique Near East.[19] I will try here to be more precise about some characteristics of this scriptural movement. The idea of religions of the Book, as we know, was launched in 1873 by Max Müller in his *Introduction to the Science of Reli-*

17. For an authoritative study, see Ephraim Elimelech Urbach, *The Sages: Their Concepts and Beliefs*, trans. Israel Abrahams (Hebrew ed. 1969; Cambridge, MA: Harvard University Press, 1979).

18. On the *minim*, see, for example, Richard Kalmin, "Christians and Heretics in Rabbinic Literature of Late Antiquity," *Harvard Theological Review* 87 (1994): 155–69.

19. Wilfred Cantwell Smith, *What Is Scripture? A Comparative Approach* (Minneapolis: Fortress Press, 1993). See further Guy G. Stroumsa, "The Scriptural Movement of Late Antiquity and Christian Monasticism," *Journal of Early Christian Studies* 16 (2008): 61–76.

gion.[20] Müller was enlarging and modernizing the Qur'anic concept of *ahl al-kitāb*. Recently adopted in a wide-ranging form by Carsten Colpe, who establishes a taxonomy of "filiations of canons" (one beginning with Israel and one beginning in India), this idea of religions of the Book merits further consideration.[21] It seems astonishing that the expression *ahl al-kitāb* has not really stimulated serious analysis.[22] In the Qur'an, the expression is in general addressed to the Jews, sometimes to the Christians, and also sometimes to both Jews and Christians. In making it a fundamental concept of its revelation, the author of the Qur'an seems indeed to be doing the work of a phenomenology of religions. As far as I know, there is no equivalent either in Greek or in Aramaic or Syriac. The Hebraic expression ʿ*am ha-sefer* (people of the Book) comes much later. In fact, neither Jews nor Christians defined themselves as "holders of the Book." The Jews had their Torah, the Christians their Gospels. For the author of the Qur'an, the concept therefore reflects the common denominator of diverse communities forming the religious mosaic of the Near East at the start of the seventh century. In a recent study, Daniel Madigan notes that the Qur'an chooses to define itself in the terms of previous religious traditions.[23] On this subject, he remarks on the importance accorded reading and/or chanting in various monastic rules, such as those written in 571 by Abraham of Koshkar, one of the great figures of Syrian monasticism. But things are more complex. If Muhammad had simply wanted to stress the fact that Jews and Christians each had their sacred book, no doubt he would have spoken in the plural, about *ahl al-kutub.* It must not be forgotten that for Muhammad

20. Max Müller, *Introduction to the Science of Religion* (London: Longmans, Green, 1873), 102ff.

21. Carsten Colpe, "Sakralisierung von Texten und Filiationen von Kanons," in *Kanon und Zensur*, ed. Assmann and Assmann, 80–92.

22. Some references are in Guy G. Stroumsa, "Early Christianity: A Religion of the Book?" in *Homer, the Bible, and Beyond*, ed. Finkelberg and Stroumsa, 153–73.

23. Daniel Madigan, *The Qur'ân's Self-Image: Writing and Authority in Islam's Scripture* (Princeton, NJ: Princeton University Press, 2001), in particular the appendix "The People of the *Kitâb*," 193–213.

the "Book" (*kitāb*) also had a precise technical meaning when he referred to *umm al-kitāb* (literally, "the Mother of the Book"), that is to say, the heavenly prototype of the divine book revealed on various occasions in the history of humanity, but never in its totality until the final revelation of the Qur'an. This book, heavenly by nature, *umm al-kitāb*, may descend onto earth, "be incarnated" as it were, but it is essentially eternal and functions as a sort of Platonic idea of the book in parallel with the created world, and to a certain degree its model. It is an oral book more than a written book. In fact, Madigan remarks that although the *kitāb* is at the heart of the perception of self belonging to Islam, *mushaf*, the codex, plays no role in its ritual. The distant origins of this conception (*umm al-kitāb*) are found in Mesopotamia, as shown long ago by the Swedish historian of religions Geo Widengren.[24] I do not have the competence to study a Qur'anic concept, but I want at least to stress the major role played by this concept in the imaginary of cultures of the Near East around the end of Antiquity. Moreover, a Jewish parallel to this concept of *umm al-kitāb* is found in a midrash that says God created the world by contemplating the book of the Torah.[25] In medieval and modern Christian thinking, too, "the great book of nature" is conceived as a divine revelation in parallel to Scripture. The importance of this concept for European intellectual history and scientific thinking is fundamental, since it constitutes the foundation of Newton's scientific effort.[26]

That the fundamental religious importance of the idea of the Book does not appear only with Islam but is present long before can be best expressed by some capital passages of the prologue to the Chapters, or *Kephalaia*, a fundamental theological text from

24. Geo Widengren, *Muhammad, the Apostle of God, and His Ascension* (King and Saviour V) (Uppsala: Lundequistska bokhandeln, 1955), in particular chapter 6, "The Heavenly Book," 115–61.

25. Genesis Rabbah 1:1.

26. Discussed in Pierre Hadot, *Zur Idee der Naturgeheimnisse: Beim Betrachten in den Humboldtschen "Ideen zu einer Geographie der Pflanzen"* (Mainz: Akademie der Wissenschaften und der Literatur, 1982).

early Manichaeism that has survived in a Coptic translation. I quote this text at length following Michel Tardieu's reconstruction.[27] Here is Mani speaking to his disciples to justify the writing down of the oral prophetic tradition:

> The world has not allowed me to write all that is in my memory. But since you are my children and my disciples, write my wisdom down entirely. . . . As for religions and sects from outside, I have also explained for each of them according to its wisdom and its Scripture, that the truth is that which I have revealed and manifested in the world. The other messengers [who preceded me] and the first fathers have revealed it in their writings. This is why I ask you with urgency that [every word], every explanation and every wisdom that I have enunciated in every place, in every town, in every region [be put into writing and gathered into books].

Mani then makes explicit his perception of the problems of "religions and sects from outside":

> [It is necessary] for you [to know, my] beloved, that when [Jesus] made his descent to the earth of the West, he had [and has] preached his hope . . . to his disciples. . . . But what had been announced by Jesus [remained unwritten]. After him, they [his disciples] wrote . . . his parables . . . and the signs and miracles. . . . [And] they wrote a book according to his. . . .
>
> (A little later:) [The messenger of] light, the resplendent illuminator, [Zoroaster, came as a] Persian to King Hystaspes. . . . [He elected] disciples righteous and truthful . . . [and he preached] his hope in Persia. [But nor did he,] Zoroaster, write a book. On the other hand, his [disciples coming] after him, remembered and wrote [books] that they read today. . . . (Finally:) When Buddha came in his turn, the [saints told us] about him that he too had preached [his

27. The text, edited and translated by Hans Jakob Polotsky, appeared anonymously in Germany under the Third Reich (1940). Michel Tardieu, "Le Prologue des 'Kephalaia' de Berlin," in *Entrer en matière: Les Prologues*, ed. Jean-Daniel Dubois and Bernard Roussel (Paris: Cerf, 1998), 65–77. See also the English translation, Iain Gardner, ed., *The Kephalaia of the Teacher: The Edited Coptic Manichaean Texts in Translation with Commentary* (Leiden: Brill, 1995).

hope and] a countless wisdom, had elected his Churches, had led
them and had revealed to them his hope. But the fact is that he did
not write his wisdom into a book and it was his disciples, coming
after him, who [remembered] a part of the wisdom that they had
heard from Buddha and put it down in writing.

In his analysis of the prologue, Tardieu stresses the great care with
which this piece is written. Jean-Daniel Dubois, for his part, sees
in the passages I have just quoted a "panorama of the history
of non-Manichaean religions" as well as the Manichaean conception of the status of Scripture "in relation to the religions
competing with Manichaeism in Iran in the time of Mani—i.e.,
Christianity, Zoroastrianism, and Buddhism."[28] Dubois forgets,
though, to signal the grand absence in this gallery of prophets:
Moses, of course. If Mani ignores Moses, this is not only due to
his deep theological anti-Semitism, which allows him to integrate in his *Heilsgeschichte* all the religions of humanity except
that of the Jews. It is also, and perhaps especially, because his argument on the degradation of the prophecy of the founders of
religions as being due to orality does not work in the case of
Moses, who remained for everybody, until Spinoza, the undis-
puted author of the Pentateuch.

The essential importance granted by Mani to the writing of
sacred texts shows to what point the Qur'anic idea of *umm al-
kitāb* (like that of the seal of prophecy, *khātim al-nabiyyīn*) develops a concept that is already found in the earliest stages of Manichaeism.[29] Like Christianity, Manichaeism expresses from the
start a universalist theology and an activist missionary practice
toward all peoples (with the exclusion of the Jews, the henchmen
of Satan, who are not integrated into the model of salvation of
humanity). Let us note that the Jewish route seems to be exactly
symmetrical, but in the opposite sense, to that of the religions

28. Jean-Daniel Dubois, "Mani, le prophète de l'humanité entière," in *Messianismes:
Variations sur une figure juive*, ed. Jean-Christophe Attias, Pierre Gisel, and Lucie Kaen-
nel (Geneva: Labor et fides, 2000), 195–212.

29. See Guy G. Stroumsa, *Savoir et salut* (Paris: Cerf, 1992), 275–88.

to which Mani refers: while the latter pass from the oral to the written, Jewish literature moves away from the written to the oral in our period. Like Christianity, too, but in a more radical way, Manichaeism proposes a theology of the translation of holy writings. The holy books of Christians were above all the sacred books of the Jews and were written in Hebrew, a language that even Christian intellectuals did not read, with very few exceptions. The philological motto of Jerome, *hebraica veritas*, was doomed to remain a dead letter.[30] As far as I know, the Byzantine millennium did not produce a single Hellenophonic Jerome, a single Christian Hebraist. In this, the Byzantines were indeed the heirs of the Greeks more than those of the Romans, with a confidence in their innate cultural superiority that prevented them from being interested in other languages and cultures, all considered barbarian—a confidence that would lead them eventually to their ruin. Even a man as intelligent as Augustine, in his correspondence with the hermit of Bethlehem, expresses his incomprehension of Jerome's pathetic efforts to master this barbarian and guttural language. Since the translation of the Septuagint is inspired by the Holy Spirit, he asks, what good is it to be preoccupied with the original?[31] This exchange, by the way, is typical of the gulf separating too often, still today, the philologist from the philosopher. In order to offer all people salvation through Christ, his revelation must be translated. Ancient Christianity thus proposes to translate the Scriptures, and with them the whole Bible, into all possible languages. Let us note that this led to the emergence of literacy for languages that had previously been only oral, such as Armenian and Gothic. It is

30. See Alfons Fürst, *Hieronymus: Askese und Wissenschaft in der Spätanike* (Freiburg: Herder 2003), 102–6. For a wide-ranging reflection on the Roman incorporation of the Hebraic dimension, see Rémi Brague, *Europe, la voie romaine* (Paris: Criterion, 1992).

31. See in particular letter 28 of Augustine to Jerome, dated 394. This correspondence was edited and annotated by Alfons Fürst, *Augustinus-Hieronymus Epistulae mutuae, Briefwechsel*, Fontes Christiani 1–2 (Turnhout: Brepols, 2002). See also Alfons Fürst, *Augustins Briefwechsel mit Hieronymus* (Münster: Aschendorffsche Verlagsbuchhandlung, 1999). I should like to thank Winrich Löhr for having drawn my attention to these works.

by these various biblical translations that Christians conserved and encouraged the plurality of religious knowledge. Thus the story of Jesus of Nazareth, and with him the whole *historia sacra* of Israel, was extended to humanity as a whole. This dynamism of Christianity that, in order to better propagate itself, encourages the translation of the Scriptures—and along with it literacy and the development of languages—shows to what extent Constantine was wrong in believing that Christianity offered him a religion fitting his empire: one god, one king, one book. Actually, Christianity encouraged competition among different linguistic and cultural centers, a fact that bears upon the phenomenon of de-globalization in Late Antiquity.[32]

The Manichaeans, however, went further in the recognition of the cultural and religious plurality of humanity, since they were not content with translating their sacred texts from Aramaic (and Pahlavi) into Coptic, Greek, and Latin, then into Uighur, Chinese, and Arabic. They offered "cultural" translations, as it were, rather than "linguistic" ones, for example, replacing their own divinities with those of the religions among which they were sending their missions. Such an option was evidently inconceivable for the Christians, for whom all religions, except that of Israel, were only idolatries, worshiping false divinities. In Late Antiquity, one may sometimes discern among some Christian authors a certain ethnological curiosity. This curiosity, though, does not go so far as to develop any sympathy for the various religions of humanity.[33] The very particular seriousness Mani granted to writing pushed him to a reform of the Pahlavi alphabet, which profoundly simplified the reading of it. Similarly, the extreme attention that the Manichaeans gave books is reflected in the

32. See Arnaldo Momigliano, "The Disadvantages of Monotheism for a Universal State," in *On Pagans, Jews, and Christians* (Middletown, CT: Wesleyan University Press, 1987), 142–58. For a different viewpoint, see Paul Veyne, *Quand notre monde est devenu chrétien (312–394)* (Paris: Albin Michel, 2006).

33. Developed in Guy G. Stroumsa, *Barbarian Philosophy: The Religious Revolution of Early Christianity*, Wissenschaftliche Untersuchungen zum Neuen Testament, no. 112 (Tübingen: Mohr Siebeck 1999), 57–84.

dialogue between text and image that they advocated by accompanying their sacred texts with illuminations.[34]

The first centuries of the Roman Empire saw a true revolution in the history of the book, its deepest transformation until Gutenberg. The Latin poet Martial, in his *Epigrams* (1.2) written between 84 and 86 of our era, has one of the first mentions of the codex.[35] From the end of the first century to that of the fourth, one can follow the systematic progress of the use of the codex, and the corollary diminution in the use of the scroll. This change in the book's aspect, at first sight purely technical, provoked a profound transformation of the role of the book and the circulation of ideas. Books were becoming more compact, easier to carry and to use, and their fabrication cost much less. Internal references were greatly facilitated. The codex allowed a rapid development of intertextuality. What is remarkable in this chapter in the technical conditions of the transmission of knowledge, rather well marked out by the papyrologists (in particular by the important work of Colin Roberts and T. C. Skeat), is the quite singular evolution of the early Christian book: here one finds practically no scrolls, even for biblical texts (only two biblical papyri do not come from codices). From the beginning, the Christians published their writings in the form of the codex.[36] At the end of the second century, the codex had become a "Christian innovation." One has even spoken of a "Christian obsession with the codex."[37] As missionaries of a *religio illicita*, the Christians were certainly interested in using compact and inexpensive books, much more practical than the traditional scrolls, and

34. See Hans Joachim Klimkeit, *Manichean Art and Calligraphy*, Iconography of Religions, no. 20 (Leiden: Brill, 1982).

35. See L. D. Reynolds and N. G. Wilson, *Scribes and Scholars: A Guide to the Transmission of Greek and Latin Literature*, 3rd ed. (Oxford: Oxford University Press, 1991), 34.

36. See Colin H. Roberts and T. C. Skeat, *The Birth of the Codex*, rev. ed. (London: Oxford University Press, 1983).

37. Robin Lane Fox, "Literacy and Power in Early Christianity," in *Literacy and Power in the Ancient World*, ed. Alan K. Bowman and Greg Woolf (Cambridge: Cambridge University Press, 1994), 126–47 and notes; see also Michael McCormick, "The Birth of the Codex and the Apostolic Life-Style," *Scriptorium* 39 (1985): 150–58.

often written less than carefully. Such a desire to circulate books
that were as small as possible is reflected in the case of the Manichaean Codex of Cologne, the smallest format codex known
in Antiquity to have survived. It is also possible that in this the
Christians wanted to dissociate themselves from the Jews, who
continued to write the Torah on scrolls.[38] Despite their tradition-
alism, the Jews were perhaps at the origin of the Christian codex, if one accepts, along with Roberts and Skeat, the suggestion
from Saul Lieberman that the Gospels find their origin in the
inscription of individual legal decisions (*halakhot*) on papyrus.[39]
In a similar way, the first disciples of Jesus rapidly adopted the
habit of noting the *logia* of their *rav* (master) and grouping them
together. However, all the practical advantages of the codex over
the scroll for the transmission of Christian knowledge do not
suffice to explain the immediate and universal character of the
use of the codex by the Christians. To break with such tradition,
they had to have weighty religious reasons. In going against all
religious and cultural norms, the Christians manifestly knew that
they were launching a genuine religious revolution: the truth, inscribed in the Book, had to reverberate as quickly and as simply
as possible, by all means, in all languages. The idea of a text sacred
down to its very letters would quickly fade (without disappearing
completely) in ancient Christianity. To a certain extent, the biblical text becomes for the Christians the technical support for the
divine word, the *Logos*.

Thus Melito of Sardis, who has been called "the first poet of
deicide," could express himself in the second century in his poem
on Easter: "And the Law became the Word [*kai ho nomos logos
egeneto*]." In a sense, one might say that the democratization of
writing in early Christianity reflects also a certain blurring of
the boundaries between the written and the oral. Thus Christian

38. This was already the explanation given by P. Katz, "The Early Christians' Use of
the Codices Instead of Rolls," *Journal of Theological Studies* 46 (1945): 63–65.

39. Saul Lieberman, *Hellenism in Jewish Palestine* (New York: Jewish Theological
Seminary of America, 1950), appendix 3, 203–8.

intellectuals learned (unlike Jewish sages) to transmit their oral teaching, also by recording it, for example, by writing down their commentaries on the Scriptures. Eusebius describes how Ambrose, Origen's benefactor, had put at his disposal a whole army of stenographers (*tachygraphoi*), copyists (*bibliographoi*), and calligraphers (in this latter case, they were young girls, *korais epi to kalligraphein ēskēmenais*).[40] The *Pastor* of Hermas, in the second century, is a good example of the desire to transmit Christian knowledge through writing. The old woman whom Hermas meets on the route to Cumes asks him to copy the little book she is reading in order to disseminate its teaching even abroad (*Vision* 2.1).

Thus the emergence of a "textual culture" in the third century seems due to a large extent to the rise of Christianity in the Roman Empire. If I am permitted an anachronistic metaphor, I propose seeing in ancient Christianity more than a "religion of the Book"—a "religion of the paperback." More than the traditional or established religions, a marginal religion like Christianity (and a little later Manichaeism) knew how to best use the new techniques of dissemination of knowledge in order to propagate itself in an effective way. Similar phenomena are of course found elsewhere. It suffices to think today of the American televangelists or the massive use of audio- or videocassettes by various radical religious movements, not only among Islamicists. Such an analysis, albeit rapid, indicates how much the hypothesis that the use of books among the Christians follows, *grosso modo*, what one might find in society at large is erroneous. Harry Gamble, in his excellent book on the subject, may err in inferring from general data to Christian communities.[41] For a long time, these communities remained, to a great extent, "enclave societ-

---

40. Eusebius *Ecclesiastical History* 6.23. See the discussion in Kim Haines-Eitzen, *Guardians of Letters: Literacy, Power, and the Transmitters of Early Christian Literature* (New York: Oxford University Press, 2000), 41–52.

41. Harry Y. Gamble Jr., *Books and Readers in the Early Church: A History of Early Texts* (New Haven, CT: Yale University Press, 1997). See further Gillian Clark, *Christianity and Roman Society* (Cambridge: Cambridge University Press, 2004), 78–92.

ies," as the sociologists say, responding to other laws than those that governed the society at large. Even if the great majority of Christians of the first centuries remained illiterate, just like in the ambient society, books played a quite different role among the Christians than among pagans.

Very early on, the Christians were keen on books. In the second century, Lucian of Samosata, in his *Peregrinus; or, The False Prophet*, mentions the Christians' many books.[42] Arrested in 180, the Christians of Scillium were brought to Carthage before the proconsul Saturninus. When he interrogated them about the content of the box they kept with them, Speratus answered in their name: "The books and the letters of Paul, a righteous man."[43] Christians, then, wrote a lot—too much, perhaps, for the taste of some. William Harris, the author of an important study of literacy in Antiquity, speaks in this respect of the "acute logorrhea of Christian authors."[44]

Above all, though, the holy book of the Christians was from the start the Septuagint, the Bible of the Jews, to which were later added the books that would form the New Testament. Augustine could write: "The Jews are our librarians, *librarii nostri*." But he called them also "guardians of our books, *custodies librorum nostrorum*."[45] The Christians were of course aware of the fact that their sacred books were those of the Jews, books that their first recipients and guardians, now blind, could no longer

42. Lucian, *Peregrine of Parion*, chap. 11. Analyzed in Christopher P. Jones, *Culture and Society in Lucian* (Cambridge, MA: Harvard University Press, 1986); and Hans Dieter Betz, "Lukian von Samosata und das Christentum," *Novum Testamentum* 3 (1959): 226–37.

43. *Acts of the Scillitan Martyrs*, 12, in Herbert Musurillo, *The Acts of the Christian Martyrs* (Oxford: Clarendon Press, 1972), 88–89. Note that books, though, remained rather rare, according to the testimony of Optatus, *Against the Donatists*, appendix 1.

44. William V. Harris, *Ancient Literacy* (Cambridge, MA: Harvard University Press, 1989). This important book, which emphasizes the differences in the roles of writing among pagans and Christians, has been discussed in Mary Beard et al., eds., *Literacy in the Roman World* (Journal of Roman Archaeology, Supplementary Series, no. 3; Ann Arbor, MI, 1991). See in particular Keith Hopkins, "Conquest by Book," 133–58.

45. Augustine *Ennarrationes in Psalmum* 56.9, *P.L.* 36:666, and Sermon 5, *P.L.* 38:52.

read and interpret correctly. Despite the harsh and often violent relations that developed in Late Antiquity between Jewish and Christian communities, the sacred books of the Jews would remain protected from destruction by fire—which was too often the fate of the sacred books of pagans (for the pagans also developed, especially later on, the idea of sacred books). Thus when in 418 the Christians of Minorca organized a pogrom against the Jewish community (and imposed a collective conversion), they burned the synagogue but insisted on saving the sacred books from the flames. In the words of Bishop Severus, who relates the incident: "The flame consumed the synagogue itself and all its decorations, except for the books and the silver. We withdrew the sacred books [*libros sanctos*] so they would not be damaged by remaining among the Jews" (note that he forgets to mention the plundering of the silver).[46] A little earlier, in 402, Christians who, under the instructions of their bishop Porphyry, destroyed the Marneion of Gaza took care to burn the sacred books of the pagans (which they called "books full of magic," *biblia peplēromena goēteias*) along with the temple and the images of the gods.[47]

The implicit theology of the Christians, then, did more than simply support the idea of translation. Not only is the *traduttore* not a *traditore*, but it may be even better to read the sacred text in translation than in the original. Here we have perhaps the deepest sense of the idea of *sermo humilis*, long ago brilliantly analyzed by Erich Auerbach.[48] One must translate the sacred texts because they are often written in a sublime language admired by cultivated people, but that does not speak equally to the simple and to the educated. Yet it is the same salvation that Christianity is trying to offer each and every person. Christian "populism" (if one

46. See Severus of Minorca, *Letter on the Conversion of the Jews*, ed. and trans. Scott Bradbury (Oxford: Oxford University Press, 1996).

47. Mark the Deacon, *Life of Porphyry*, chap. 71.

48. Erich Auerbach, "Sermo humilis," in *Literary Language and Its Public in Late Latin Antiquity and in the Middle Ages*, trans. Ralph Mannheim, with a new foreword by Jan M. Ziolkowski (Princeton, NJ: Princeton University Press, 1993). The article first appeared in 1941.

might say that) is at least in theory an exaggerated populism that runs against the best established cultural instincts: for the Christians, the simple and rugged prose of sinners is preferable to the pure and sublime language of the poets. Origen's *Contra Celsum*, for example, clearly expresses this violent opposition, reflecting a contrast less between two opposite theologies than two fundamentally different conceptions of the very idea of religion.[49] In his polemical work *Against the Galileans,* Emperor Julian expresses the same contemptuous disdain toward the vulgar language of the Gospels, in itself a weighty argument against their sacred character. Let us note here that the Islamic concept of *i'jaz al-Qur'an,* the "inimitability [of the language] of the Qur'an," would reflect the same attitude. Its unequaled poetic beauty proves the divine origin of the sacred text.

In the traditional cultures of the ancient world, on the contrary, the very idea of translation was something worrying. The *Letter of Aristeas* that recounts the legendary story of the translation of the Septuagint reflects the traditional suspicion when it insists on the miraculous nature of this translation.[50] A Hermetic text, *From Asclepios to King Amon* (*Corpus Hermeticum* 16.1–2) returns to the dangers of translation in the case of Egyptian into Greek, this time with a more radical attitude. For the Hermetic author, the Greek language is incapable of expressing the profound mysteries that the Egyptian language succeeds in presenting in a clear fashion. Unlike Greek, which with its false graces succeeds only in producing empty discourse, Egyptian uses "sounds full of efficacy." Thus Asclepios recommends to the king trying to prevent as much as possible the translation into Greek of Egyptian books. The power of the Egyptian language is of course that of the hieroglyphs, "symbols under which are hidden

---

49. See Stroumsa, *Barbarian Philosophy*, 44–55.

50. For a recent study of this text, see Sylvie Honigman, *The Septuagint and Homeric Scholarship in Alexandria: A Study in the Narrative of the Letter of Aristeas* (London: Routledge, 2003).

the mystagogy," as they are described by Iamblichus in his *Mysteries of Egypt* (8.1).

Around the 180s, Irenaeus is our first witness to the idea of a collection of Christian texts grouped under the name New Testament (*kainē diathēkē*). Of course, the canon of the New Testament would not be finally fixed until the fourth century, but it is accepted that by the end of the second century the concept was there. It probably made its first appearance in the context of the conflict with Marcion, the first author to differentiate between authentic and inauthentic Christian writings (and of course rejecting en masse the writings of the Old Testament) around the 140s. Rivers of ink have been spilled over the problem of how the Christian canon was constituted, right back to the *Decretum Gelasianum* at the end of the fifth century or the beginning of the sixth, with its list *de libris recipiendis et non recipiendis*. I certainly cannot pretend to take up the question here, but I would like to note one fact generally passed over in silence.

The text of the Mishnah ("repetition," understood as "of the Torah," *deuterosis* in Greek) was fixed by Rabbi Judah, called the Prince, more or less at the end of the second century (and the start of the third) and is thus almost contemporaneous with the beginning of the idea of the New Testament canon. Strangely, this synchrony does not seem to have been noticed. It might be a matter of a coincidence, but this is not very probable. The intellectual struggles of the second century that would result in the crystallization of Christian identity did not take place only against the dualists of all kinds whom we usually call loosely the "Gnostics." Alongside fighting heresy and writing apologetics, the first Christian intellectuals devoted a good part of their efforts to the conflict between *vetus* and *verus Israel*. Throughout the second century, Jewish-Christian polemic represented an essential aspect of Christian literature in its struggle for a defining identity. In a period traumatic for all parties, where imperial power was persecuting some and violently repressing the revolts of others, Jews and Christians alike were engaged in a dramatic process of "orthodoxization." And since the contention between the two communities turned essentially around the correct interpretation of the same Scriptures, each side developed, in intense competition with the other, a key for this interpretation that was specific to it and to which the other community did not have access. I propose seeing in the New Testament, on the one hand, and the Mishnah, on the other, the most concrete fruits of this competition.[51] In both cases, it is a matter of a secondary text, "new" or "a repetition." This text has no meaning unless read in parallel with the Scriptures, which, for their part, only find their real significance through the prism of the new text. The two corpuses thus reflect the distancing of the two religions from each other in their fundamental structures, one putting the accent on prophetic faith, the other on ritual practice. But for both Jews and Christians, it was a matter of offering a key to actualizing the Scriptures for a hermeneutic community for which they were the law. It seems to me this is how we must understand the famous dictum of Martin Buber that the Old Testament is for the Jews neither old nor a testament.

The biblical contention between Jews and Christians, however, was not close to disappearing, as witnessed by the famous Novella 146 of Justinian, a law promulgated in Constantinople in February 553.[52] This Novella—whose title, *Peri Hebraiōn*, seems to allude to the Hebreophony of the Jews (who would otherwise have been called simply *Ioudaioi*)—banned the Jews from reading the *deuterosis* in Hebrew. It seems that Justinian was referring here to the Mishnah. In effect, Hebrew represented the principal advantage of Jews over Christians in understanding Scripture. The inspiration of the Septuagint could not completely eliminate a certain feeling of inferiority vis-à-vis those who were reading the sacred text in the original. Justinian's argument here is that the

---

51. See Stroumsa, *Hidden Wisdom*, 79–91.

52. Text and translation in Amnon Linder, *The Jews in Roman Imperial Legislation* (Detroit: Wayne State University Press, 1987), 402–11.

Jews should not adhere to the letter of the biblical text but rather recognize the prophecies that it contains. We should not believe, though, that the Novella indicates a solid knowledge of Hebrew among Byzantine Jews around the middle of the sixth century. What it reflects, as Leonard Rutgers argues, is the "hermeneutic Jew," the Jew inside the head of the Christian emperor.[53] What causes fear about this imaginary Jew is the power that his knowledge of the original language of the Scriptures confers on him. Mastery of knowledge in general, and of the content of books in particular, is conceived of as an instrument of power—a power not only intellectual but also magical. In Late Antiquity, the magical power of books is often linked to the unknown language in which they were written. Here Hebrew has a choice place, amply demonstrated in magical Greek papyri. Hebrew names or words of Hebraic consonance are there to recall the hieratic power of *nomina barbara*. Thus, entire meaningless phrases are bewitching in the enigmatic resonance of their strange sounds. In similar fashion, we find in several Hebrew texts of Late Antiquity some words of Greek consonance that were placed there to give local color or intellectual justification.

In effect, books were often used as talismans. We know the vogue for *sortes evangelicae*, described by Augustine among others. But the pagans practiced the same kind of rituals, opening the books of Virgil to read the future in them. For Servius, a contemporary of Jerome, and for Macrobius, Virgil is practically a sacred author. The victory of Christianity in the fourth century brought some pagans to develop similar attitudes, or at least parallel ones. The books used for the cult of Marnas in Gaza, and burned in an auto-da-fé organized by Bishop Porphyry at the start of the fifth century, are only one example among many others of pagan ritual books, prescriptive and descriptive texts of

53. Leonard Rutgers, "Justinian's Novella 146, between Jews and Christians," in *Jewish Culture and Society under the Christian Roman Empire*, ed. Richard Kalmin and Seth Schwartz (Leuven: Peeters, 2003), 385–407.

rituals of all kinds. Think, for example, of the famous (and mis-named) "Mithras Liturgy" of the great magic papyrus of Paris.[54] A simple note about the auto-da-fé: Let us not assume that this was a Christian invention; Roman power also occasionally erected pyres of Christian and Manichaean books. Pierre Chuvin, who mentions these facts, comments: "The triumph of the Book has some sinister backlashes."[55] Let us add that such facts underline how erroneous is the common conception that makes religious intolerance an invention (or at least a specialty) of monotheistic religions. We will return to this point in chapter 4.

Perhaps the most remarkable case of the desire among some pagans to have "sacred books" is the fate of the *Chaldean Oracles* in late Neoplatonism. The *Chaldean Oracles*, that amalgam of insipid verses written in the second century by a certain Julian and addressed to the chthonic goddess Hecate, became in the fourth century a sort of bible, a sacred text about which allegorical commentaries were written. Marinus tells us in his *Life of Proclus* that his hero put above all other books the *Chaldean Oracles* and Plato's *Timaeus*, asserting that these are the only two books he would leave in circulation "if he were master."[56]

Proclus reveals himself here as an authentic student of the totalitarianism that Karl Popper discerned in Plato. The scriptural movement of Late Antiquity, let us not forget, also represented one of the terrains over which there was a merciless battle for power, intellectual and religious as much as political. The processes of canonization among the sages of Israel and among the Church fathers were also, as we have seen, processes of exclusion and censorship. Since neither the Jews nor the Christians were in the first centuries anywhere near imperial power, these struggles over texts reflect the combat within both these communities for

54. See Hans Dieter Betz, *The "Mithras Liturgy": Text, Translation, and Commentary* (Tübingen: Mohr Siebeck, 2003).

55. Pierre Chuvin, *Chronique des derniers païens* (Paris: Les Belles Lettres, 1990), 165.

56. On the *Chaldean Oracles* and their influence, see Hans Lewy, *Chaldean Oracles and Theurgy: Mysticism, Magic, and Platonism in the Later Roman Empire*, new ed. by Michel Tardieu (Paris: Études augustiniennes, 1978) (1st ed. 1956).

religious power. The line separating permitted books from forbidden books follows the moving frontier between the orthodoxy that is being constituted and heresy under its multiple forms.

I mentioned above a taxonomy of religions of the Book in Late Antiquity according to the status granted to the book and to reading. It is clear that the Jewish attitude toward the sacred book and its place in theology and in worship—toward its use in magical rituals, the possibility of its translation, and the modes by which it should be interpreted—differs from what we find among Christians, Manichaeans, various Baptist or so-called Gnostic sects, the Neoplatonists, and in emergent Islam. The literary form of the text and the language in which one reads it or uses it in public and private worship, according to the milieus' structures and the norms of its teaching, all differ according to communities and cultural milieus. Finally, authority passes into new hands. The rabbis, the fathers, the monks, and the saints all represent so many new forms of religious authority. Each of these groups lives with sacred texts, reads them, and uses them in a different way.

The great Orientalist Theodor Nöldeke, glory of the University of Strasbourg under the Second Reich, conceived of Islam as the form that Christianity had taken among the Arabs. Perhaps we must modify this vision of things. Islam, rather, represents the result of the interaction among the various religious movements in the Near East of Late Antiquity. It indeed seems that the Qur'an, which stands outside my enterprise here, remained, at least during a short period of a few decades, an oral book (a virtual one, we would say today), before it was written down. It was thus a text of incantatory accents that received its force from chanting, the natural form of reading it—a sometimes strange text in some of its concepts, as in its vocabulary and grammar, and foundational (in the most direct sense) of both Arabic language and Muslim thought. Here we see that the deep transformation of reading under the Roman Empire—corollary of the shift from scroll to codex, interiorizing itself by the shift from reading out loud to silent reading—does not find a precise parallel in early Islam. Such a transformation would happen a little later with the urbanization of the new conquering religion.

In alluding to silent, interiorized reading, we are touching a very important domain that should at least be mentioned here: esoteric traditions in the religions of Late Antiquity. Plato, in his *Seventh Letter*, had already dealt with the dangers of writing, which becomes quickly uncontrollable as that writing circulates. The most essential doctrines, then, can only be divulged to a small group of disciples and must remain oral. In the religious systems that we are examining, the dialectic between oral traditions and written texts follows an axis parallel to the complex relations between esoteric and exoteric traditions. We rediscover these relations everywhere, but in different forms and with different intonations. All ancient religions seem to have possessed esoteric dimensions, reserved for an elite. Judaism and Zoroastrianism resemble here Mediterranean mystery religions. It is Christianity that first encounters a serious contradiction between its fundamental ethos, which offers salvation to everyone without any preference for intellectual and religious elites, and the idea of esoteric traditions that are found in the first stages of Christianity. The Gnostic traditions are the *locus classicus* for finding esoteric traditions, which are Jewish (or Jewish-Christian) in origin. It is precisely because they were so well implanted in the fertile soil of dualist sects that these esoteric traditions were quickly eradicated from Christian teaching. Thus in the fourth century, when the pagan danger was perceived by some Christian intellectuals as belonging to the past, we may observe, with the birth of a mystical literature in the patristic tradition, the secondary use (as the archaeologists say) of the vocabulary of vanished esoteric traditions.[57]

With the Christianization of the empire, the whole education system was being transformed. Arguing from the fact that the Christians could not teach Homeric texts since the mythology repelled them, Emperor Julian had in 361 banned Christians

57. See Stroumsa, *Hidden Wisdom*, passim.

from the teaching profession, the same profession that had been forbidden to Christians by Tertullian for the same reason. Still in the third century, the *Didascalia Apostolorum* required "abstaining completely from pagan books." But in the fourth century, Christians were forced to become the link in the transmission of the Hellenic culture that they had decried so much. Thus, Basil of Caesarea, Gregory of Nazianzus, and John Chrysostom all wondered as teachers about the legitimate way of reading and teaching the pagan classics to the young.

If the Christianization of the empire did not lead to a radical iconoclasm and to the destruction of pagan literature, it was precisely because Christian identity crystallized around the faith in the message of translated Scriptures, hence detached from their original ethnic or cultural tradition. In the monasteries, in the East as well as in the West, the text of the Scriptures, the sole foundation of monastic culture, was uninterruptedly read, copied, learned, commented upon, chanted, and translated.[58] In the great urban centers of the East, on the other hand, Christians succeeded rather easily in Christianizing Greco-Roman teaching, or rather in establishing and developing a double culture, pivoting around the two totally different literary traditions, but that would together constitute what I propose calling the "double helix" (in reference to the DNA structure discovered by Francis Crick and James Watson).[59] The Bible and some of the great classical texts of Greco-Latin culture—especially those coming from the Stoic and Platonic traditions, which seemed to suit the Christians (*Seneca saepe noster*)—together formed the double foundation of Byzantine culture and medieval Latin culture. The Christian hermeneutic revolution, which had already added the New Testament to the Old by postulating that one could not be understood without the other, now proposed applying the same system, *mutatis mutandis,* to the two cultural corpuses of Athens

58. See Douglas Burton-Christie, *The Word in the Desert: Scripture and the Quest for Holiness in Early Christian Monasticism* (New York: Oxford University Press, 1993).

59. Stroumsa, *Barbarian Philosophy,* 27–43.

and Jerusalem. Tertullian had claimed in vain that there could be nothing in common between the two cities. Christians constituted themselves as a culture by integrating both the culture of Israel and that of Greece. A new dignity was now attributed to silent reading by the sage, both scribe and theologian. This silent reading, as we have seen, inaugurated a new relation to the text, and even a new form of worship, private and interior. It thus permitted the development of perhaps the most remarkable difference between the religions of the Book and ancient religions: the place reserved for theology at the very heart of religion. In Greece, philosophical thinking had been conceived as reflection on religion, critical or not, but remaining in any case outside it.

This was a turning point of decisive importance that would structure all of Western thinking from Philo to Spinoza, who put a final stop to the identification, or collusion, between philosophy and theology. From the Cappadocians to John of Damascus in the East, from Augustine and Jerome to Cassiodorus and Isidore of Seville in the West, Christian culture was constituted by sliding from biblical hermeneutics to cultural hermeneutics. After the reappropriation of Jewish Scripture, Christianity effected an appropriation of Greco-Roman culture, subordinating *logos* to *pistis*. This fundamental process had already been described by Augustine in *De doctrina Christiana*, where he spoke of recuperating "the riches of the Egyptians" (2.40.60).

Reading and writing coincide in the practice of monasticism, as shown by Guglielmo Cavallo.[60] But reading and interpreting also coincide. Reading, liturgical chanting, writing, translation, commentary, copying: the work of the Book, the gathering of books, represents one of the most profound cultural but also religious transformations between Antiquity and the Middle Ages. From the scroll to the codex, reading has become intensive rather than

---

60. See p. 29 n. 3, above. See also *On Virginity; or, On Acsesis* 1.12, attributed to Athanasius, preaching the continual practice of the Scriptures. Translated by T. M. Shaw, in *Religions of Late Antiquity in Practice*, ed. Richard Valantasis (Princeton, NJ: Princeton University Press, 2000), 82–99.

extensive. In the textual communities par excellence of the monasteries, one reads few books but one often learns them by heart. In Late Antiquity, the radical simplification of mythology is not only that of the pantheon; it is also that of the library, organized now around a single book, which provided the fundamental hermeneutic principle of all intellectual wealth. Patristic and monastic thought here rejoins the Jewish ethos, which had transformed the Greek *paideia* into a supreme religious value: *ein ʿam ha-aretz ḥassid.* "The ignorant person cannot be pious" (*Avot* 2:5).

3

Transformations of Ritual

The psychological and cultural transformations with which we have dealt to this point simultaneously permitted and imposed a series of deep restructurings of the very idea of ritual in various religious contexts. The preceding chapter has shown how the rise of the religions of the Book transformed the attitude to religious stories, that is, to myths. It stands to reason that one can identify a corollary transformation of the very idea of ritual. Throughout history, as Philippe Borgeaud has noted, the fabulatory function and the ritualistic function constantly recomposed their fundamental interrelation, redefining religion as an agent of identification.[1] New perceptions of individual purity, both bodily and moral, and a new form of *historia sacra* in place of myths would impose new approaches to religious *activity* in the Mediterranean and Near Eastern world during the first centuries of the common era.

I have already noted the weak heuristic value of the tradi-

1. Philippe Borgeaud, "La mémoire éclatée: À propos de quelques croyances relatives au mythe," in *Théories de la religion*, ed. Pierre Gisel and Jean-Marc Tétaz (Geneva: Labor et fides, 2002), 221.

tional taxonomy that insists on a division between polytheistic and monotheistic systems. Sacrifices, especially blood sacrifices, underline this point. In the ancient world, they were in effect at the very heart of religious activity, certainly of any public and official religious activity, both among Jews and pagans. Thus, Emperor Julian, called the Apostate, could write in the second half of the fourth century:

> The Jews conduct themselves like Gentiles [*tois ethnesin*] except that they recognize only one God. This is something particular to them that is foreign to us. For the rest, however, we share the same ground— temples, sanctuaries, altars, rituals of purification, and some injunctions where we do not diverge from each other—or else only in an insignificant way.[2]

There is no need to accept the total mimetic theory of René Girard to grant him the primordial character of the institution of sacrifice in ancient cultures.[3] But our period is distinguished by an upheaval in the equilibrium between myth and ritual that had been maintained by sacrifices in ancient societies.

Sacrificiorum aboleatur insania: "That the folly of sacrifices be abolished," states a law of Constantius II.[4] We could characterize the revolution begun by Constantine and pursued by his successors by focusing on one of its most radical consequences: the end of public sacrifices. But one precision is necessary: even the imperial *fiat* could not eradicate an institution as profoundly embedded as sacrifice. As Walter Burkert remarks, "Even the religious revolution of the Near East represented by Islam did not succeed in eliminating animal sacrifice"; Islam devoted a festival

2. Julian, *Against the Galileans*, fragment 72. For a comparative study of Greek and Jewish sacrificial practices, see Maria-Zoe Petropoulou, *Animal Sacrifice in Ancient Greek Religion, Judaism, and Christianity, 100 BC–AD 200* (Oxford: Oxford University Press, 2008).

3. See in particular René Girard, *Le Sacrifice* (Paris: Bibliothèque nationale de France, 2003), 48.

4. Theodosian Codex 16.10.2. See Nicole Belayche, "Le sacrifice et la théorie du sacrifice pendant la 'réaction païenne': L'empereur Julien," *Revue de l'histoire des religions* 218 (2001): 455–86.

to sacrifice, giving it its name, "*Id al-adhā.*"[5] To a certain extent, then, sacrifice would remain present even after its official death. But the trenchancy of Burkert's remark is misleading: animal sacrifices in Islam as well as relics of sacrifices found in Christianized societies show that they had a status quite different from sacrifices in Roman imperial religion. Thus Frank Trombley has offered a precise analysis of the *Ritenchristianisierung* (the Christianization of rites) in Late Antiquity Anatolia and Greece.[6] And for his own period, dealing with the claimed survival of animal sacrifice in some rituals of Christianized societies of the High Middle Ages in the West, Cristiano Grottanelli showed recently to what extent they were different, in both structure and function, from the pagan animal sacrifices they were supposed to be perpetuating.[7] On the other hand, the measures taken by Constantine in 317–21 in favor of the Church and its clerics did not encroach upon public religion. Let us not forget that Constantine remained *pontifex maximus.* Thus public worship financed by the state continued normally, even under Constantius II, though he was the author of famous laws against sacrifices.[8]

Well before the interdiction of sacrifices around the end of the fourth century, however, one could follow a great debate within Hellenic thought about the necessity and value of sacrifices. On this subject, there was a profound change in sacrificial ritual, the linchpin of the pagan system, which was transformed from an alliance between the community and its gods into the preparation of a mystical experience. Thus prohibition of animal sacri-

---

5. Walter Burkert, *Homo Necans: The Anthropology of Ancient Greek Sacrificial Ritual and Myth* (German ed. 1972; Berkeley: University of California Press, 1983), 11.

6. Frank R. Trombley, "Paganism in the Greek World at the End of Antiquity: The Case of Rural Anatolia and Greece," *Harvard Theological Review* 78 (1985): 327–52.

7. Cristiano Grottanelli, "Tuer des animaux pour la fête de saint Félix: Paulin de Nole et la boucherie sacrée, *Carmen XX*," in *La cuisine et l'autel: Les sacrifices en question dans les sociétés de la Méditerranée ancienne*, ed. Stella Georgoudi, Renée Koch Piettre, and Francis Schmidt (Turnhout: Brepols, 2005), 387–406. See also Cristiano Grottanelli, *Il sacrificio* (Rome: Laterza, 1999).

8. See Nicole Belayche, "*Realia versus leges?* Les sacrifices de la religion de l'État au IVe siècle," in *La cuisine et l'autel*, ed. Georgoudi, Piettre, and Schmidt, 343–70.

fices occurred while they were "less in favor among the pagans."[9] The evolution of ideas about sacrifice among pagan intellectuals is well-known and has no need to be recalled here in detail, and so I would simply like to note certain high points in this evolution. Lucian of Samosata, that Voltaire of the second century, is the author of an essay on sacrifices, a Cynic diatribe of sorts (*Peri thusiōn*). Lucian begins by noting that whoever observes religious practices (sacrifices, festivals, processions, prayers, beliefs) could only laugh at seeing the stupidity (*tēn abelterian*) of all these activities. Further on, he notes that the poor man who cannot pay for the luxury of an animal, or even a cake, to offer the god instead contents himself with paying homage by kissing his own hand. Describing the priest splattered with the blood of an animal groaning while its throat is slit to music, he adds sarcastically: "Who would not suppose that the gods love to see all that?" The Scythians, for their part, thought animals too vile and preferred to offer men to Artemis![10]

Writing in the final third of the third century, Porphyry bases his criticism of sacrifices on a whole tradition deriving from the *Peri eusebeias* of Theophrastus, for whom animal sacrifices represented a perversion of the true Greek religious tradition.[11] For Porphyry, it is the philosopher who is the true priest of the supreme god. He serves this god, above all, by his temperance, his *sophrosynē*, which allows him to approach God with a pure body and soul. The real temple is the sage's thought (*tēn dianoian malista tou sophou monēn*); the sage transforms his heart into an altar upon which reigns the real statue of God, the sage's in-

9. Pierre Chuvin, *Chronique des derniers païens* (Paris: Les Belles Lettres, 1990), chap. 14, "Une ferveur nouvelle," in particular 237–44. On Roman sacrifices, see John Scheid, *Quand faire, c'est croire: Les rites sacrificiels des Romains* (Paris: Aubier, 2005); see also Francesca Prescendi, *Décrire et comprendre le sacrifice: Les réflexions des Romains sure leur proper religion à partir de la littérature antiquaire* (Potsdamer Altertumwissenschaftliche Beiträge, 19; Stuttgart: Franz Steiner Verlag, 2007).

10. See the text and A. M. Harmon's translation in Loeb Classical Library, *Lucian*, vol. 3 (Cambridge, MA: Harvard University Press, 1960), 155–77, see esp. 166.

11. On the sources for Porphyry, see the introduction to Porphyry, *De l'abstinence*, trans. Jean Bouffartigue and M. Patillon (Paris: Les Belles Lettres, 1979), vol. 2, p. 9.

tellect.[12] In his treatise *On Abstinence*, one of the most interesting philosophical books of the age, Porphyry develops his views on the relations between philosophy and asceticism. The title indicates above all abstinence from meat. The philosopher owes it to himself to be vegetarian, thus isolating himself from the civic community, "whose cohesion is affirmed around the altar with the smoke of the victims offered by the *polis* to its gods,"[13] as Jean Bouffartigue writes. For the Theophrastian tradition of criticizing sacrifices, then, civic religion rests on an infraction of divine law, or on a poor interpretation of it. Let us note the particular place accorded by Theophrastus, and in his wake by Porphyry, to animal sacrifices among the Jews. These sacrifices are very different from those of the Greeks, for the Jews do not consume the meat offered to their God but burn up the victims entirely. The Greeks, though, carefully avoid imitating them on this point! For the Jews are a "race" of philosophers: their sacrifices are just so many occasions for maintaining divine things, "and at night they contemplate the stars, gazing at them and calling on God in their prayers."[14] If the Jews were offering blood sacrifices, it was not under the impulse of their appetites that they did so, like other peoples, but rather because they were pushed by necessity. This necessity, writes Porphyry (after Theophrastus), was famine, which once pushed men to cannibalism and later was transformed into human sacrifice, whereas the original sacrificial practice by humanity had been purely vegetal. Animal sacrifices represent a later phase than human sacrifices.[15]

The philosopher, who is thus also a historian of religions, understands that "we must, then, be joined and made like [god],

<hr />

12. *Letter to Marcella*, 11, quoted in Porphyry the Philosopher, *To Marcella*, trans. Kathleen O'Brien Wicker (Atlanta: Scholars Press, 1987), 54–55.

13. Introduction to Porphyry, *De l'abstinence*, trans. Bouffartigue and Patillon, vol. 2, p. LXII. See also Alberto Camplani and Marco Zambon, "Il sacrificcio come problema in alcune correnti filosofiche di età imperiale," *Annali di Storia dell' Esegesi* 19 (2002): 59–99.

14. Porphyry *On Abstinence from Killing Animals* 2.26.3. I quote the translation by Gillian Clark (Ithaca, NY: Cornell University Press, 2000), 65.

15. Ibid., 2.27.1.

and must offer our own uplifting as a holy sacrifice to [him], for it is both our hymn and our security. This sacrifice is fulfilled in dispassion of the soul and contemplation of the god."[16]

The current to which Porphyry lends his powerful voice is of course not the only one among Hellenic intellectuals. For traditionalists like Emperor Julian, who were opposed to any innovation (*kainotomia*), in particular with regard to the religious laws given by the gods to our ancestors and that we have received as an inheritance, blood sacrifices were to be preserved without hesitation.[17] But even among the intellectual apologetes of sacrifices, one can discern a clear evolution in ideas and a questioning of their ontological value. Iamblichus, for example, deals with sacrifices (shortly before Julian) in book 5 of his *Mysteries of Egypt*. Opposing Porphyry's vegetarianism, he says that superior beings have no need of sacrifices; for they are suited only for material gods. Blood sacrifices represent the material aspect of the cult, but worship rendered to the gods should also be spiritual. It is the dual condition of man, material as much as spiritual, that imposes this cultic duality. Alongside the blood sacrifices, there is thus another sort of sacrifice that is spiritual.[18] These spiritual sacrifices are those offered by philosophers, who rise toward the One beyond the crowd of divinities: a small elite that is above any law. Therefore blood sacrifices are the ones imposed on the hoi polloi, on all those who need a lawgiver (chapter 22). Toward the end of book 5, Iamblichus deals with prayer in sacrifice (chapter 26). In its three degrees, prayer has the goal of bringing us closer to the gods, of introducing contact with the divine. Sacrifice and prayer mutually reinforce each other.

Union with the gods is also at the center of the catechism of late paganism embodied in the small book *Concerning the Gods and the Universe*, written by Sallustius, Julian's teacher. For Sallustius,

16. Ibid., 2.34.3; Clark trans., p. 69.

17. Julian, *Letter 20* to Theodorus, 453b.

18. Iamblichus, *Les Mystères d'Égypte*, ed. and trans. E. Des Places (Paris: Les Belles Lettres, 1966), 5.15, 169–71.

even if the temples are so many veritable copies of the heavens and the very script of indescribable heavenly powers, the gods have nothing to gain from these temples (what could the gods gain?)—but as for us, there we can find union (*sunaphè*) with them.[19]

Blood sacrifices represent our own lives, which we are symbolically offering. And prayers detached from sacrifices are worth nothing, because they are nothing but words, whereas if pronounced during sacrifices, they become animated words, *empsychoi logoi*. The soul that leaves the sacrificed animal in some way ascends to heaven with the words of prayers in which we ask for union with the gods (chapter 16). Thus we see that even among the keenest defenders of sacrifices, they do have a new function, oriented less toward conservation of collective identity than toward transformation of the individual identity.[20]

Since before the end of the first century CE, the Jews (much against their will) had offered the example of a society that had succeeded in conserving its ethnic and religious identity, even after the destruction of the only temple where daily sacrifices could be offered. For the historian of religions, the sudden disappearance of sacrifices in a community represents a deep transformation of the very structures of its religious life. And yet the Jews in the first centuries of our era, both in the Roman Empire and in Babylonia (in the Sasanian Empire after the third century), succeeded in the gamble of transforming their religion in a radical way. They "modernized" it, as it were, without seeming to, by pretending (and sometimes believing) that they were changing nothing essential. For this was indeed a modernization of religion, due to the new accent placed on interiorization and privatization of worship.[21] Among the Jews, as in other commu-

---

19. Sallustius, *Concerning the Gods and the Universe*, ed. and trans. Arthur Darby Nock (Cambridge: Cambridge University Press, 1926; repr., Hildesheim: G. Olms, 1966), chap. 15, 28–29.

20. See Chuvin, *Chronique des derniers païens*, 257.

21. See chapter 4, below. On the transformation of the concept of worship, see Bernhard Lang, "Wie sagt man 'Kult' auf Lateinisch und Griechisch? Versuch einter Antwort anhand antiker und christlicher Texte," in Christoph Auffarth and Jörg Rüpke,

nities, sacrifice was replaced, above all, by prayer. The new religious status of the word gives it a power of action: to say is now to do, to use the title of a classic of modern philosophy, John Austin's *How to Do Things with Words*. To be sure, this transformation, critical for the religious and cultural history of Europe, took place only slowly and jerkily.

Still, one can assert without paradox that more than any other singular action, it was the destruction of the Temple of Jerusalem by Titus in 70 CE, as a result of the Jewish revolt, that activated the slow—overly slow—transformation of religion to which we owe, among other things, European culture. The Jews should no doubt pay thanks to Titus, whose memory they hold in contempt, for having destroyed their temple for the second time, for imposing on them the need to free themselves from sacrifice and its ritual violence, before any other society. "Despite themselves" because they seem to have been immediately seduced by the offer made to them by Julian, a new Cyrus, to reconstruct their temple more than three centuries after its destruction.[22]

The destruction of the Temple of the Jews after practically a millennium of existence and activity was bound to have consequences, both direct and indirect, which are still far from having been well identified and analyzed. One of these consequences, of course, was the creation of not one, but at least two new religions: Christianity alongside rabbinic Judaism, and also various dualist currents that are usually called Gnosticism.[23] Here we note— and will return to it later—that to a certain extent rabbinic Judaism and Christianity would both remain sacrificial religions, but very special sacrificial religions because they functioned without

---

eds., *Epitomē tēs oikoumenēs: Studien zur römischen Religion in Antike und Neuzeit* (Stuttgart: Steiner, 2002), 29–36.

22. On this episode, see the texts gathered by Menahem Stern, *Greek and Latin Authors on Jews and Judaism*, vol. 2 (Jerusalem: Israel Academy of Science and Humanities, 1980).

23. See Michael A. Williams, *Rethinking "Gnosticism": An Argument for Dismantling a Dubious Category* (Princeton, NJ: Princeton University Press, 1996).

blood sacrifice.[24] The rabbis did not ever deny the primacy of the Temple, and Jewish historiosophy will always come back to the idealized golden age of Palestinian Jewish society gathered around its temple. Between the past imaginatively invented and the messiah who will restore it, the Jews lived in an expectation rather similar to that of Parousia for the Christians, the return of Christ, who is both priest and sacrifice according to the Epistle to the Hebrews. Moreover, Christ in early Christian eschatology—for example, with Irenaeus—was supposed to lead from the Temple Mount in Jerusalem the final battle against the Antichrist.[25]

Another consequence of the destruction of the Temple in Jerusalem is that it permitted the spiritualization of the liturgy, *leitourgia,* by transforming rites accompanying sacrificial activity, by prayers replacing the daily sacrifices, and by giving ancient prayers a value that they had not previously had.

The destruction of the Temple did not imply only what I have just called "spiritualization"—as ambiguous as the term may be, and which I am using (without any value judgment) to indicate the shift to a ritual without priests and without blood sacrifices. We know of the attraction sometimes exerted by Judaism in certain high social classes of Roman society in the first and second centuries, an attraction going sometimes as far as conversion, or at least to that sort of "Judaism for free auditors" or "fellow travelers" represented by the "God-fearers," *yr'ei shamaim* or *phoboumenoi.*[26] In philo-semitic milieus, sometimes even within the imperial family, the Jews were perceived as a race of philosophers among the peoples of the Near East, who were called generically "Syrians." They were a race of philosophers

---

24. See the various articles on sacrifice (*Opfer*) in *Die Religion in Geschichte und Gegenwart,* 4th ed., 6.570b–593a.

25. See Irenaeus *Adversus Haereses* 5.20–25; the last chapters of the book. See also Stefan Heid, *Chiliasmus und Antichrist-Mythos: Eine frühchristliche Kontroverse um das Heilige Land* (Bonn: Borengässer, 1993).

26. See Bernd Wander, *Gottesfürchtige und Sympathisanten: Studien zum heidnischen Umfeld von Diasporasynagogen* (Tübingen: Mohr Siebeck, 1998).

not only on account of their monotheism, but also, it seems to me, for their worship without sacrifices, hence more spiritual. Numenius of Apamea, a neo-Pythagorean thinker who around the middle of the second century called Plato an "Atticizing Moses" (*Mousēs attikizans*), is undoubtedly one of the key people in this philo-semitic movement,[27] but one finds similar admiring statements until the third century, for example, in Porphyry's *De abstinentia*, to which I alluded above. What matters from the present perspective is that the Jews—a people whose ways of worship had been destabilized, and who in order to survive had to practically reinvent their religion, or at least their ritual—might offer under the High Empire the very example of a spiritualized religion, or a religion without blood. The horror of blood, and hence of sacrifices and also (directly linked to sacrifices) of meat, which was displayed by several pagan intellectuals—Porphyry among others—may also perhaps have a Jewish component, at least indirectly.

An additional consequence of the destruction of the Temple of Jerusalem is the democratization and spatial explosion of Jewish worship. The Temple of Jerusalem owed its celebrity to its uniqueness. The end of sacrifices also brought the disappearance for all useful purposes of the caste of priests (*kohanim*) and of their Jerusalemite monopoly. Jewish ritual was now no longer linked to a sacred space, to the *omphalos* represented by the Temple. It could take place anywhere, with anybody. The rabbis are teachers, but they are not priests and have no liturgical role. A group of ten adult men may constitute a community and may without any other condition celebrate public worship. God, who has lost his palace, his own habitation, now "stays with the locals," as it were. The divine presence, the *shekhina* (from the root *shakhan*, to inhabit) whose specific place had been in the Temple, is now found (according to a well-known midrash) in "the four cubits of the *halakha* alone."[28] Note that the idea of *shekhina* seems

---

27. See Stern, *Greek and Latin Authors on Jews and Judaism*, 2:206–16.
28. Babylonian Talmud, *Berakhoth*, 8a. *Halakha* refers to religious law.

to develop only after the destruction of the Temple: who in fact would have worried about the divine presence before the catastrophe of 70 CE? It was evident that God inhabited the Temple as his own, which is where he was at home. The *shekhina* was limited to the four cubits of the *halakha*: here we manifestly observe a privatization of religion, passing from the most official and public status of *religio civilis* to the quiet rituals of individual and familial religion.

If God is no longer in the place that was his by nature, one might wonder how it was possible to see him. By tradition, of course, the God of the Jews had particular whims: he did not let himself be seen, not even in his temple, which did not contain his statue, unlike the temples of other gods; he did not even let himself be named, under pain of death, and one had to use pseudonyms to call upon him. His power was such that any infraction of these interdictions could lead to immediate death. A god without statues, with an unspeakable name: is it so astonishing that the Jews were so often considered, prior to the Christians, as atheists?[29]

One may legitimately ask the question of how aware the Jewish intellectuals of the first centuries of our era were of their revolutionary situation in relation to the sacrificial religion of the Temple. The Mishnah and other rabbinic texts, in particular the treatise *Berakhoth* (Blessings) of the Talmud, discuss the reinterpretation of Temple traditions.[30] We may discern three attitudes among the rabbis: the first insists on the natural advantage of the era when the Temple was standing over the contemporary period, when one has to be content with ersatz sacrifice. This

29. See Guy G. Stroumsa, "A Nameless God: Judaeo-Christian and Gnostic 'Theologies of the Name,'" in *The Image of the Judaeo-Christians in Ancient Jewish and Christian Literature*, ed. Peter J. Tomson and Doris Lambers-Petry (Tübingen: Mohr Siebeck, 2003). 230–43. This essay is reprinted in the second edition of my *Hidden Wisdom: Esoteric Traditions and the Roots of Christian Mysticism*, Studies in the History of Religions, no. 70 (Leiden: Brill, 2005), 184–99.

30. Marcel Simon, *Verus Israel: A Study of the Relations between Christians and Jews in the Roman Empire (135–425)* (French ed. 1947; New York: Oxford University Press, 1986) remains a classic. See the first chapter.

attitude reflects a clear impression of religious decadence. The second attitude that can be found in rabbinic literature does echo, in all its ambiguity, the radical reorganization of a Judaism that is reconstituting itself into a religion without sacrifices. Finally, the third attitude conveys an impression of superiority over the past: for the sages, who consider themselves somewhat the equivalent of philosophers in Greco-Roman society, the study of the Torah, the *Talmud Torah*, has replaced sacrifices. As we have already seen, the study of the Torah represents Jewish acceptance of the Greek value of the *scholē*. Witness the ten *batlanim*, literally "men of leisure" or even "gentlemen scholars" (in modern Hebrew, by a misfortune of semantic evolution, "good-for-nothings," "loafers")—individuals without a job other than studying—whose presence according to the Mishnah defines a town as opposed to a village. Supported by texts, Michael Satlow has recently shown how *Talmud Torah* replaced sacrifice among the rabbis.[31]

Among rabbinic sages, unlike among the Church fathers, the rejection of metaphor imposed the urgency of new terms and conceptions upon which the new religious system could be founded. The rabbis had succeeded in constructing a system in which individual daily praxis—the closed network of behavior according to the law, *halakhah*, and also, for the elites, hermeneutic reflection—has replaced the order of sacrifices. This transformation stressed the *story* of sacrifice, whose reactivated memory has now been invested with a new power. Ritual was transformed into the story of ritual—into myth, in a way. The system of *halakhah* framed life in such a way that one could rightly speak of a Jewish equivalent of the *askēsis* of philosophers and Christian elites.[32]

31. Mishnah, *Megillah*, 1.3. Michael I. Satlow, "'And on the Earth You Shall Sleep': *Talmud Torah* and Rabbinic Asceticism," *Journal of Religion* (2003): 204–25.

32. See Ephraim Elimelech Urbach, *The Sages: Their Concepts and Beliefs* (Hebrew ed. 1969; Jerusalem: Magnes Press, 1975), chap. 13; and also Urbach, "Ascesis and Suffering in the Thought of the Sages," in *The World of the Sages* (in Hebrew) (Jerusalem: Magnes Press, 2002), 437–58.

These three attitudes are often found mixed with each other, sometimes in the same people. The liturgical prayer that replaces sacrifices receives a new status that reproduces the daily rhythm of sacrifices: morning and afternoon, not counting the additional sacrifice (*mussaf*) of the Sabbath and festival days. This prayer includes various texts mentioning sacrifices, either biblical verses, usually taken from Leviticus, or else various Mishnaic texts dealing with sacrifices. Telling has replaced the doing to such a point that the recitation in a synagogue of sacrificial injunctions is now equivalent to their former practice in the Temple. One injunction, conserved in the *Shulhan Arukh*, the great legal code written in the sixteenth century, goes so far as to prescribe the death penalty (rhetorical, of course) for an error in the recitation of the biblical injunctions on the burning of sacrifices, just as the death penalty was required, in the era when the Temple was in existence, for errors concerning the ritual itself.[33]

Rav Shesheth, referring to the animal fat and blood burned in sacrifice, compares them to the fat and blood burned during a fast, a fast that equals a sacrifice by its power to atone for sins.[34] Alongside praying and fasting, charity replaces Temple liturgy. Thus in the third century, Rabbi Eleazar ben Pedat, a Babylonian sage who had emigrated to Palestine, says: "To do charity and justice is more acceptable to the Lord than sacrifice," adding in categorical fashion: "Prayer is higher than sacrifice."[35] Prayer, fasting, and charity thus become the three pillars enabling the reconstitution of religion and hence the survival of the world after the fall of the Temple.

For the same Rabbi Eleazar, the destruction of the Temple brought about the construction of a wall of iron (*homat barzel*), a veritable "barrier of separation" between Israel and its God.[36] This wall implies that the links between God and the people of Israel

33. *Shulhan Arukh, Orah Hayim, Hilkhot nefilat apayim*, 133.

34. Babylonian Talmud, *Berakhoth*, 17a.

35. Babylonian Talmud, *Sukkah*, 49b.

36. Babylonian Talmud, *Berakhoth*, 32b. See Baruch M. Bokser, "The Wall Separating God and Israel," *Jewish Quarterly Review* 73 (1983): 349–74.

have now lost the naturalness that was theirs when the Temple existed. The "iron curtain" that separates us from the numinous requires that we present our requests to the heavenly power without expecting from it an immediate or obvious response. Thus it is a religion of alienation, of the absence of God, that was invented by the sages of Israel after the end of sacrifices. The divine presence is no longer, as in the Temple, evidence that it is sufficient to *evoke*; one can now only *invoke* it. In such conditions, we perhaps understand how one can speak of the modernization of religion and of its interiorization. As with patristic thought, one may also refer to *Entzauberung*, or disenchantment: the link to the divine is no longer evident or immediate (far from it).[37] Therefore religious practice is distanced from the principle *ex opere operato* that was the natural mode according to which sacrifices functioned. Under the old regime of sacrifices, religious action in itself had had the power, or at least the ambition, to engage divine power, since it affirmed the equilibrium of the world and the link between the divine and human worlds. Now it is the individual consciousness that is charged with constantly reinvigorating the relation with the divine, still more invisible and incomprehensible than when the Temple was standing. Ideally speaking, prayer, fasting, and charity are all practiced in silence and in secret, and also without any certainty of recompense. The religious practice of the Jews, just as much as that of Christians, is defined now (at least in theory) by supererogation: the new practice can indeed replace sacrifices. It is the contrite heart and the intention, both invisible by nature, that God appreciates.[38] In this sense, we see how the religiosity of the sages relays that of the prophets: it was not the smoke or odor of sacrifices that pleased God, said the sages. Now there is no longer the smoke or the smell of grilled meat, which might form an illusion. Thus the religion of intention invented by the prophets is adopted by the sages,

---

37. See the analysis of this concept in Guy G. Stroumsa, *Savoir et salut* (Paris: Cerf, 1992), 163–81.

38. Babylonian Talmud, *Sanhedrin*, 106b.

who make it the foundation of their orthodoxy. This orthodoxy is not limited (as is often said) to an orthopraxy, even if the field of belief and its place in the definition of identity are very removed from their centrality in patristic thought.

Let me open a parenthesis on method. It is far from evident that before the fifth century the sages represented much more than themselves. In Palestine, at least, it seems that the great majority of Jews were content with a less ideological religiosity, and one that was certainly more syncretistic than the elitist system of the rabbis. It was only later, in a perhaps paradoxical way with the Christianization of the empire, and in particular with that of a Palestine now transformed into the Christian Holy Land, that the rabbis managed to impose their authority over the Jewish communities, even in Palestine.[39]

In a recent book, Rachel Elior has taken up the question of the origin of mystical traditions in ancient Judaism.[40] She proposes locating it among Zadokite priests excluded from worship by the Hasmonaean usurpers in the second decade of the second century BCE. The expelled priests, according to her, took refuge in Qumran with their library, developing a whole series of cogitations centered around ideas of the Temple, of divine palaces (*hekhalot*), and the divine chariot (*merkavah*) described in the first chapter of Ezekiel. She says it is only after the destruction of the Temple, however, that these cogitations would be transformed into the texts called, precisely, the literature of the *hekhalot* and *merkavah*, which represents the core of early Jewish mystical literature. Alongside the divine palaces and the chariot, some Hebrew texts of Late Antiquity deal with the cosmic body of God, giving fantastic dimensions to his limbs (literature called *Shiur Qoma*, of the "dimension of [his] size").[41]

---

39. Here I accept the central argument of Seth Schwartz, *Imperialism and Jewish Society, 200 B.C.E.–640 C.E.* (Princeton, NJ: Princeton University Press, 2001).

40. Rachel Elior, *The Three Temples: On the Emergence of Jewish Mysticism* (Oxford: Littman Library of Jewish Civilization, 2004).

41. See Gershom Scholem, *Jewish Gnosticism, Merkavah Mysticism, and Talmudic Tradition* (New York: Theological Seminary of America, 1960).

That the development of Jewish mysticism is linked to the Temple's destruction is not hard to believe: mystical ambitions, sometimes going as far as *unio mystica* for the elites who culti-vate them, relate to a strong religious experience, like that which, at least in theory, Temple offerers of sacrifice might have had. Mysticism, even if it is by definition a limited movement, rep-resents an opening up of religion: such an experience of the di-vine presence is no longer reserved for priests, but is offered to the new religious elites (sages, Gnostics, or saints). What is still more remarkable, however, is the fact that such traditions about the vision of the Body of God, of his palace(s) and his chariot, are found in various early Christian texts. Earliest Christian lit-erature, as we know, echoes Jewish apocalyptic traditions, like the Apocalypse of John describing the splendors of heavenly Jerusalem. And so the transformation of the spatial representa-tion effected by the new absence of the Temple is found in early Christianity. "The person who knows himself is both *topos* and *thronos*," we read in the *Homilies* of Pseudo-Macarius, an East-ern Greek text of the fourth century that would deeply influence Western Christian mysticism until the modern era.[42] The soul of the mystic is the divine throne, the divine glory (*kavod, doxa*), and the divine presence itself is the *shekhina*. *Topos*, the site, is an appellation for the Temple as well as for God (*ha-maqom*, "place" in Hebrew). That such traditions are found in some of the Gnos-tic texts from the early second century is not surprising. These texts, in fact, retain for us some esoteric Jewish traditions that, accepted by Jewish-Christians and applied to their new concep-tions, would be quickly rejected by the Christian intellectual cur-rents that would form patristic orthodoxy. But these traditions would become the foundation of Christian mystical thinking. To give only a few examples, let me mention the *Book of Elcha-sai* (of which we have only traces in the heresiological literature) and the *Resurrection of Jesus Christ by the Apostle Bartholomew*,

42. See the introduction of George Maloney to his translation of Pseudo-Macarius, *The Fifty Spiritual Homilies and the Great Letter* (New York: Paulist Press, 1992).

which echoes these traditions rather clearly. The *Vision of Doro-theus*, a recently published Greek papyrus in the Bodmer Collection, preserves a vision of the divine palace by a Christian author of the fourth century. The isomorphisms between such texts and the Jewish traditions mentioned above are striking enough to deserve a comparative analysis.[43]

Various Greek and Syriac texts of Late Antiquity offer arresting parallels with some Jewish texts, thus revealing among Jews and Christians, especially to the East, and among the Byzantines as under the Sasanians, similar attitudes toward the mystical and interiorized reinterpretation of the powerful religious experiences of the priest in the Temple.

What do the Christian texts tell us about the topic of sacrifice? In some of its aspects, early Christianity represents a transformation of Judaism that opens it to new horizons, but it seems in other ways to mark a conservative return to Israel's sacrificial system. While the rabbis gathered in Yavneh in 70 succeeded in transforming Judaism—without admitting doing so, and perhaps also without admitting it completely even to themselves—into a non-sacrificial religion, Christianity defined itself precisely as a religion centered on sacrifice, even if it was a reinterpreted sacrifice. The Christian *anamnēsis* was the reactivation of the sacrifice of the Son of God, performed by the priests.[44] Christianity is also a religion of priests, and hence of ecclesiastical hierarchy, not of sages who are in principle equal in their knowledge and their power. It is a religion without a temple, then, but a religion in which sacrifice is offered, or re-offered, perpetually. The very fact of the metaphorization of biblical traditions allows them to con-

43. See Guy G. Stroumsa, "To See or Not to See: On the Early History of the *Visio Beatifica*," in *Wege mystischer Gotteserfahrung/Mystical Approaches to God*, ed. Peter Schäfer (Munich: Oldenburg, 2006), 67–80. I am of course aware of the dangers of what one could call "parallelomania"; noting symmetries or parallels should not replace identifying influences. Moreover, even the proven influence of one concept on another belonging to a different religious tradition does not necessarily imply that the same theme functions in an identical or similar way in the two contexts.

44. See Jean-Claude Basset, "L'anamnèse: Aux sources de la tradition chrétienne," in *La mémoire des religions*, ed. Philippe Borgeaud (Geneva: Labor et fides, 1988), 91–104.

serve at least the *terms* of the religion of Israel. One can follow, in the patristic authors' liturgical language, the clear development of a sacrificial vocabulary that increasingly asserts its continuity with the ancient tradition.[45]

Among the Christians of the first centuries, the ascetic praxis of the *imitatio Christi* takes a radical form, expressing the will to go up to martyrdom in order to repeat in some way the sacrifice of the Son of God, a sacrifice that had also been, in theory, the last of human sacrifices. Of course, human sacrifices form a separate category in the taxonomy of sacrifices and in their study. They are not simply blood sacrifices like the others. Under the Roman Empire, for every author who refers to human sacrifices, they represent the very frontier between humanity and barbarity.[46] The repulsion proclaimed by Christians for sacrifices in general, and their horror at human sacrifices in particular, would play a significant role in the eradication of human sacrifices in the Mediterranean world. Yet we know human sacrifices were practiced much longer than one might want to believe, since Tertullian, among others, mentions their existence in the province of Africa at the start of the third century.[47] Both Clement of Alexandria and later Eusebius assert that only Christianity succeeded

45. See in particular Robert J. Daly, *Christian Sacrifice: The Judaeo-Christian Background before Origen* (Washington, DC: Catholic University of America Press, 1978); Frances M. Young, *The Use of Sacrificial Ideas in Greek and Christian Writers from the New Testament to John Chrysostom* (Cambridge, MA: Philadelphia Patristic Foundation, 1979); and Everett Ferguson, "Spiritual Sacrifice in Early Christianity and Its Environment," *Aufstieg und Niedergang der römischen Welt II* 23, no. 1 (1980): 1151–89. See also Gerd Theissen, *A Theory of Primitive Christian Religion* (London: SCM Press, 1999), chap. 8, "The Sacrificial Interpretation of the Death of Jesus and the End of Sacrifice," 139–60. Theissen characterizes the early Christian abandonment of sacrifices as "a revolution in the history of religion" (139). See George Heyman, *The Power of Sacrifice: Roman and Christian Discourses in Conflict* (Washington, DC: Catholic University of America Press, 2007).

46. See James B. Rives, "Human Sacrifice among Pagans and Christians," *Journal of Roman Studies* 85 (1995): 65–85. See further Jan N. Bremmer, ed., *The Strange Way of Human Sacrifice* (Leuven: Peeters, 2006).

47. On the Christian polemic against sacrifices, see, for example, Marco Rizzi, "Il sacrificio pagano nella polemica dell'apologetica Christiana del II secolo," *Annali di Storia dell'Exegesi* 18 (2001): 197–209.

in putting an end to human sacrifices.[48] But this horror of human sacrifices went hand in hand with an acceptance of martyrdom, sometimes even with an attraction toward it. In the first Christian texts outside the New Testament, those of the Apostolic and Apologetic fathers, a great importance is accorded to sacrifice. The sacrifice of Christians is above all the Eucharistic liturgy, of course. Thus the *Didache*, around the year 100: "And on the Lord's day, after you have gathered, break the bread and offer the Eucharist, having confessed your sins, so the sacrifice may be pure" (14:1–2). Such an approach quickly becomes the common perception and the very definition of the Eucharist. One may note, moreover, the gradual reinforcement of sacrificial vocabulary in Christian liturgical language. Thus, around the end of the fourth century, John Chrysostom—who will become one of the pillars of orthodoxy and whose influence will remain major across the centuries, in the West as in the East—writes:

> Do we not offer a daily sacrifice? We do, but as a memorial [*anamnēsis*] of His death. Why, then, is it a single sacrifice rather than multiple sacrifices? . . . We always offer the same person, and not one sheep today and another one tomorrow, but always the same offering. . . . There is a single sacrifice, and a single high priest who has offered the sacrifice that purifies us. Today, we offer what has already been offered, an inexhaustible sacrifice. This is done as a memorial of what was done then, for he said: "Do this in memory of me." We do not offer another sacrifice, as was once done by the high priest, but we always offer the same sacrifice—or rather, we re-present it.[49]

In a metaphoric mode, Christian sacrifice is also "a contrite heart," starting in the second century.[50] Prayers offered by Christians are the only perfect and God-pleasing sacrifices.[51] Such a conception of prayer as sacrifice is found as far away as the Syriac

48. Clement *Protrepticus* 3.42; Eusebius *Praeparatio Evangelica* 4.16.10.

49. John Chrysostom, *Homilies on the Epistle to the Hebrews*, 17.3 (on Hebrews 9:24–26), *P.G.* 63, col. 131.

50. Clement of Rome, *Epistle to the Corinthians*, 52.

51. Justin Martyr, *Dialogue with Trypho*, 117.1–3.

writer Aphrahat, the "Persian Sage" of fourth-century Mesopotamia (*Demonstration 4*). Also in Mesopotamia there developed, still in the fourth century, a movement of Christian ascetics who insisted on the idea of continual prayer as the only effective means of preventing the domination of Satan over the world. For these Euchites or Messalians, these "beseechers" according to their Greek or Syriac name, continual prayer replaced (as at Qumran) the daily sacrifice, in Hebrew *qorban tamid*, literally "perpetual sacrifice."[52]

Ignatius of Antioch, in the first two decades of the second century, went further. In his *Epistle to the Romans*, he specifically identifies his future martyrdom with a sacrifice offered to God (chapter 2), saying that his flesh as it is devoured by wild beasts will be transformed into the "pure bread of Christ" (chapter 4). The martyr is someone who testifies, like a seal, *sphragis*, to the authenticity of the message of Jesus, we are told by Polycarp, the first to use the word *martys* in that way.[53]

In a study as brilliant as it is suggestive, *Martyrdom and Rome*, Glen Bowersock has shown, against a whole historiographic tradition, that the Christian martyrs in Rome reflected an attitude quite different from that of the Maccabean martyrs.[54] The identification of the martyr with a sacrifice seems to me to support Bowersock's thesis in another way. In effect, it is only in a situation in which the sacrifice offered in the Temple no longer exists that such a metaphoric acceptance of the term might be developed. The *Martyrdom of Perpetua and Felicity* (18.4) seems to me one of the most gripping testimonies of the perception of the martyr as a sacrifice, as much by the pagans as by the Christians. At the circus, before confronting the beasts, the Christians

---

52. On the origins of continual prayer, see Ithamar Gruenwald, "Angelic Songs, the Qedushah, and the Problem of the Origin of Hekhalot Literature," in *From Apocalypticism to Gnosticism* (Frankfurt: P. Lang, 1988).

53. *Martyrdom of Polycarp* 14.2.

54. Glen W. Bowersock, *Martyrdom and Rome* (Cambridge: Cambridge University Press, 1995). For a different approach, see Daniel Boyarin, "Martyrdom and the Making of Christianity and Judaism," *Journal of Early Christian Studies* 6 (1998): 577–627.

are made to dress in the robes of the priests of Saturn (for the men) and of the priestesses of Ceres (for the women). The ritual, even carnivalesque, character of the execution of Christians here transforms the circus into a temple. Pagans seemed to oblige the Christians, who offered themselves voluntarily as human sacrifices, contrary to even their most solid beliefs. In his *Peri stephanōn* (4.9–72), the Christian Latin poet Prudentius conceives of the martyr's death as a sacrifice, both redemptive and purifying. Such a concept echoes what Origen wrote. Referring to John 1:29 ("Behold the Lamb of God who takes away the sin of the world"), Origen notes that the Old Testament speaks of the sacrifice of five animals. Four of these five animals, for him, prefigure the martyrs. Before Prudentius, Origen seems to be the only one to make this parallel between the sacrificial texts of the Old Testament and the Christian martyrs.[55]

The art historian Jaś Elsner has recently shown to what extent the formal transformation of art from Augustus to Justinian expresses an incorporation in Roman culture of subjectivity into its very structure.[56] Elsner shows in a convincing way how Mithraism, Neoplatonism, and Christianity all moved between the end of the second century and the end of the third in the same direction, toward the "symbolic" mode. The image of Mithras, for example, no longer represents the god itself but rather the *symbol* of the god. Insisting on the fact that one has to conceive of Christianity, too, as a sacrificial religion, Elsner analyzes the mosaics of Santa Maria Maggiore in Rome dating from Pope Sixtus III, in the 430s, and the sacrificial processions in the mosaics of Sant'Apollinaris Nuovo. According to him, these mosaics demonstrate not only the symbolic polysemy of Christian sacrifice, but also the radical abolition of the ideology of reciprocity, even if the pagan gesture of sac-

---

55. See. J. Petruccione, "The Martyr Death as Sacrifice: Prudentius, *Peristephanon* 4.9–72," *Vigilae Christianae* 49 (1995): 245–57.

56. Jaś Elsner, *Art and the Roman Viewer: The Transformation of Art from the Pagan World to Christianity* (Cambridge: Cambridge University Press, 1995). See in particular chapter 2, 157ff.

rifice was still known. The martyrs and virgins no longer bring the sacrifice—they *are* the sacrifice. In effect, Christianity offers to every man and woman the possibility of becoming the sacrifice. If art here has the function of offering exegesis that allows the celebrant to understand his act, these mosaics reflect the profound transformation of religious action between pagan Rome and Christian Rome. The representations of sacrifice thus reflect a fundamental conceptual break in the very meaning of religion.[57]

In the shift from the offerer to the offering, one discerns a radical transformation of religious conduct, which must have had aberrant consequences. This transformation seems not to have been quite understood and explained. Since a historian of ancient religions is also a citizen of the modern world, he or she is allowed to reflect on the contemporary phenomenon of "suicide bombers," men and women as bombs, ready for martyrdom by their own hands—but on condition of killing as many humans as possible, in Jerusalem, New York, or Moscow today, perhaps tomorrow in Tokyo, Barcelona, or Paris. One may refer here to the extraordinary document to which historians of religions should pay the greatest attention: the notes of Muhammad Atta, the terrorist leader on September 11, 2001, which were found with his effects at the Boston airport. Atta describes in Arabic for his personal use, with icy precision, stage by stage, the rites to perform in his mission for the greater glory of God.[58] We have here, clearly, a kind of "Islamicized" ritual of a human rather than an animal sacrifice that must be performed in a state of physical and spiritual purity (purity described in precise terms) and without the "priest" letting himself be carried away with feelings of anger

57. See Guy G. Stroumsa, "Les martyrs chrétiens et l'inversion des émotions," in *Aspect émotionels de la violence*, ed. Philippe Borgeaud (Recherches et recontres; Geneva: Presses de l'Université de Genève, forthcoming).

58. I cite here according to Hans Kippenberg and Tilman Seidensticker, eds., *Terror im Dienste Gottes: Die "Geistige Anleitung" der Attentäter des 11. September 2001* (Frankfurt: Campus, 2004). See further Bruce Lincoln, *Holy Terrors: Thinking about Religion after September 11* (Chicago: University of Chicago Press, 2003).

or compassion, right to the act of slaughtering the flight atten-
dant in the captured airplane, as if it were a matter of a sheep of
the *'Id al-adḥā*. Here it is the ritual action (and it alone) that has
a soteriological value, overthrowing the order of the world and
ipso facto offering paradise to the new sacrificed sacrificer. Note
that unlike animal sacrifice, where the beast was supposed to ac-
quiesce in its death, here such acquiescence is not asked of the
sacrificed humans.[59]

One is able to discern, among Christians as among Jews, a
fundamental ambiguity vis-à-vis the very idea of sacrifice, an
ambiguity that demands we define Judaism and Christianity as
sacrificial religions without blood sacrifices. It is no less true that
for the Christians, the destruction of the Temple of Jerusalem
quickly signified a heavenly punishment inflicted on the Jews for
the crime of deicide. In Christian eyes, the sacrificial system of
Israel was defunct, terminated forever; pagan sacrifices, cults offered to demons, had evidently no value whatsoever. They were
religious fossils of a past that should be changed under the new
covenant. Christian thinkers to a large extent recognized the novelty of the system they were in the course of fashioning. This
awareness of their originality allowed them, as of the first half of
the second century, to develop a new conception of the history
of religions. For Christians as for Jews, the history of religion
was not part of history. It was rather general history that was integrated within the framework of the *Heilsgeschichte*, the history
of salvation. Toward the end of the second century, Clement of
Alexandria was perhaps not among the most innovative of the
Christian theologians, but his intellectual curiosity about reli-

59. See, for instance, Jan N. Bremmer, "Scapegoat Rituals in Ancient Greece," in
Oxford Readings in Greek Religion, ed. Richard Buxton (Oxford: Oxford University
Press, 2000), 271–93. See further Bremmer, "The Scapegoat between Northern Syria,
Hittites, Israelites, Greeks and Early Christians," in *Greek Religion and Culture, the Bible
and the Ancient Near East*, Jerusalem Studies in Religion and Culture, no. 8 (Leiden:
Brill, 2008), 169–214. For a very perceptive analysis of the transformation of sacrifice in
early Islam, see Christian Décourbet, "La fin du sacrifice," in *Le mendiant et le combat-
tant: L'institution de l'islam* (Paris: Le Seuil, 1991), 341–55.

gious phenomena, which might be compared to that of his elder, the pagan Lucian of Samosata, makes him one of our most precious witnesses about various "mystery" cults (as a Christian, it did not bother him to violate their arcana) and also about Egyptian religion in its final phases. In his *Protrepticus*, Clement offered what one might call a concise history of paganism in seven stages, trying to explain the theological errors of both Greeks and barbarians.[60] For several Christian thinkers, moreover, the sacrifices formerly offered in the Jerusalem Temple represented a concession permitted by God to a stiff-necked people, overly influenced by the practices of pagan peoples such as Egyptians, among whom they had long sojourned. For these theologians, perhaps influenced by the Theophrastic tradition to which I alluded above, biblical sacrifices represented only a stopgap, conserving the whiffs of paganism, and destined to be replaced by the new covenant. Note that toward the end of the twelfth century, the Arabic-speaking Jewish philosopher Maimonides, who thought of himself as responsible for a community of individuals incapable of attaining intellectual truth, developed in his *Guide for the Perplexed* a historical conception of sacrifices that seems literally copied from the one invented by the Church fathers and that also echoes certain of Iamblichus's ideas (although we cannot retrieve the channels through which it passed from Christian authors to Maimonides).[61] Whatever the case, this historicizing and relativizing reflection on biblical sacrifices would in turn be passed along at the start of the modern era to some Christian scholars who were trying to reflect rationally both on the biblical text and on the comparative history of ancient religions. To give only one example, but a major one, let me mention John Spencer

60. See Guy G. Stroumsa, "Cultural Memory in Early Christianity: Clement of Alexandria and the History of Religions," in *Axial Civilizations and World History*, ed. S. N. Eisenstadt, J. P. Arnason, and B. Wittrock, Jerusalem Studies in Religion and Culture, no. 4 (Leiden: Brill, 2004), 293–315.

61. See Sarah Stroumsa, "Sabéens de Haran et Sabéens de Maïmonide," in *Maïmonide, philosophe et savant*, ed. Tony Lévy and Rushdi Rashed (Louvain: Peeters, 2004), 335–52.

and his *De legibus hebraeorum ritualibus*, dating from 1684. One thus sees how patristic reflection on the end of sacrifices had a dramatic historical influence; it would even be rediscovered, at the end of a complex itinerary, in the origins of the modern discipline of the history of religions.[62]

The fall of the Jerusalem Temple that put an end to Jewish sacrifices naturally allowed early Christianity to slide the center of its magnetic field from Jerusalem to Rome: *Romam factam Hierosolymam* (Rome become Jerusalem), as Jerome would rather hastily put it. Christianity wanted almost from its beginnings to be a religion at the level of the empire at least. As Christian Jerusalem was becoming a metaphor on the model of sacrifice, situated in heaven, so now (just as sacrifice belonged to the past) a thorough reorganization of religious space and religious time became necessary. The urgent Messianic expectation of Parousia became blurred and the world was losing its axis, its *omphalos*. The capital of the empire, being also that of idols, could not really become God's capital, and it was elsewhere that Christians had to establish their true citizenship. Thus Augustine, after the sack of Rome by Alaric in 410, felt the need to explain to overly worried Christians that Rome, city of paganism, merited heavenly punishment and that in no case could the *civitas Dei* be identified with the *civitas terrena*. I cannot insist enough on this overthrow of the categories in which the very idea of religion had been inscribed until then. In their Diaspora, the Jews had succeeded in reorganizing a religious life without daily Temple sacrifices. But a diaspora without a center is no longer a diaspora. The disappearance of a locatable central focus must have had long-term capital importance for the Christian perception of the relation between religion and the state. The kingdom of God being no longer of this world, according to the Gospels, the ambiguity would remain total, through the centuries of Caesaropapism, in the East as in the West. Once again we see how the end of sacri-

---

62. See Guy G. Stroumsa, "John Spencer and the Roots of Idolatry," *History of Religions* 40 (2001): 1–23.

fice in the Temple of Jerusalem brought with it a transformation, deep and durable, in both the nature of worship and its place in the economy of the world.

I have dealt here less with transformations in the pagan sacrificial ritual, in particular the imperial cult, which imposed its very structure on the *oikoumenē*, than I have with the avatars of Jewish ritual as celebrated in small provincial towns on the confines of the desert. If I have done so, it is because we have not sufficiently appreciated the weight, in the Mediterranean world of the first centuries of our era, that was possessed by the suggestive power of marginality, in the example of a non-sacrificial ritual, even if it came from a rebel and foreign people, on the one hand, and communities outside the law, on the other.

Treating the status of sacrifices among pagans, Jews, and Christians, I have mentioned a fundamental ambiguity: the practice of sacrifice does not want to die, and thus sacrifice appears at once terminable and interminable. I briefly referred above to the theory of René Girard that Christianity put an end once and for all to the sacrificial violence of all the religions of Antiquity. One can easily detect the theological echoes, or the pseudo-theological flavor, of such a theory: the religion of the love of men is also that of the blood of Christ. We know the evocative power and terrible force of the blood painted on statues and images—even still quite recently. We can imagine how this power and this force, amplified by today's cinema, still risks calling for blood, since it is true that the pious evocation of Christ's sacrifice does not lead to repentance alone.

For the Crucifixion is indeed a matter of sacrifice. For the Jews who were the first Christians (before they were even called so), two possibilities were open in order to interpret the Crucifixion of the Messiah. Like Paul, one might accept this paradox and transform it into the lever of faith in the suffering servant— after all, a figure known in ancient Judaism. But one might also refuse the ignominious death of the Son of God. Such an attitude, we know, represents one of the oldest and most radical of Christian heresies, Docetism: Jesus did not die on the cross; he only appeared (*dokein*) to suffer; his blood was not shed. In a second stage, amalgamating with Platonic concepts, Docetism came to deny the corporal nature of Jesus. Several Gnostic and Docetist texts and traditions from the start of the second century describe a Christ laughing in heaven at seeing poor Simon of Cyrene crucified in his place, knowing that the plan of the powers of evil had been defeated. There is no need to be Christian to be shocked by such an idea. Until now this laughter of Christ has not been explained—a laughter that of course had nothing to do with the one of which Lucian spoke. I think I recently found a plausible explanation for this laugh.[63] The idea that the blood of the human victim was not spilled, that the sacrifice had been avoided at the last moment, was of course a central idea in Jewish consciousness: this was exactly what had happened to Isaac, whose sacrifice had not been performed. The binding of Isaac, his *Aqeda* in Genesis 22, was a theme of central importance in first-century Jewish imagination. Much later, when this binding became a sacrifice, it remained a key theme in patristic thought and also in Christian representations, as is shown by the ubiquity of the scene on sarcophagi. Isaac, indeed, quickly becomes in Christian thought a *typos*, or a *figura* of Christ, and his "sacrifice" a *sacramentum futuri* of the future Passion of Christ, with the obvious difference that Isaac was not killed on the altar like Jesus on the cross. That Jews who believed Jesus was the Messiah could have interpreted his binding on the cross as similar (in its consequences as well) to the *Aqeda* of Isaac should not be doubted. Thus the laughter of Christ seems to make direct allusion to the biblical etymology of the very name of Isaac, *yzḥak*, "he will laugh." Numerous Jewish and Christian texts support this argument. Here I refer to Philo of Alexandria, who comes back several times to the significance of the name Isaac. At some

63. See Guy G. Stroumsa, "Christ's Laughter: Docetic Origins Reconsidered," *Journal of Early Christian Studies* 12 (2004): 267–88. My proposal is further developed in Ronnie Goldstein and Guy G. Stroumsa, "The Greek and Jewish Origins of Docetism: A New Proposal," *Zeitschrift für Antikes Christentum/Journal of Early Christianity* 10 (2006): 423–41.

point, he even adds, using the esoteric language of the mystics and announcing the revelation of a great secret, that Isaac was not, contrary to appearance, the son of Abraham, but rather of God! The maternity of Sarah is not in doubt, but Philo believes he knows that God, before giving birth to Isaac, miraculously returned Sarah to virginity.[64] Thus we have from a contemporary of Paul's the idea that Isaac was the son of God and of a virgin! The texts are irrefutably there and yet nobody seems to have discussed them. How can one explain why such a tradition does not seem to have been remarked upon and interrogated, except because it is quite simply too "huge" and overthrows too many firm convictions?

From our perspective, the fact is that the Pauline interpretation, which will win the upper hand in the combat against the Docetist interpretation, insists on seeing the Crucifixion as a veritable sacrifice that was carried out right to the end. Sacrifices may well have ceased at the Temple of Jerusalem, and three centuries later in all temples of the empire, but the idea of sacrifice (and with it, violence) was manifestly far from dying.[65]

64. Philo *De Cherub* 42–51. See also *Quod Det.* 124, *Mut. Num.* 131.

65. As this book was going to press, I read the very important article of Ekaterina Kovaltchuk, "The Encaenia of St. Sophia: Animal Sacrifice in Christian Context," *Scrinium* 4 (2008), 161–203. Kovaltchuk shows animal sacrifice to have been a current phenomenon in Christian context, both in the East and in the West, in Late Antiquity and in the Middle Ages.

4

From Civic Religion to Community Religion

With the exhaustion, prohibition, and finally quasi-extinction of sacrificial rites, the very idea of ritual purity would evidently be put to a rude test. It would emerge radically transformed, around the end of Antiquity. After the prophets of Israel, Jesus had already questioned the absolute value of rituals of purity by insisting that it is what comes out of the mouth that soils, rather than what enters it. The water of ablutions and baptism had replaced for Christians and for Jews the fire of sacrifices. For Porphyry, as we have seen, the soul is the interior temple; rituals of purity were becoming the rules of asceticism. As for Mani, his rejection of the ancient systems of purification, to which he denied any efficacy, was more radical: neither fire nor water can efface the stains that are inherent in our very corporality.[1]

In ancient systems, sacrifices were generally performed in public, in sight of everyone, and above all were supposed to maintain

---

1. For an analysis of this rejection, its context, and implications, see Guy G. Stroumsa, *Barbarian Philosophy: The Religious Revolution of Early Christianity*, Wissenschaftliche Untersuchungen zum Neuen Testament, no. 112 (Tübingen: Mohr Siebeck 1999), 268–81.

collective identity. If the idea of, and need for, sacrifice did not disappear as totally as was once believed, the temples would be well and truly destroyed in the iconoclastic violence of the Christian triumphalism of the fifth century, all around the Mediterranean.[2] The end of official animal sacrifices implies the end of the civic rituals and the public festivals upon which the power of Rome relied in the provinces. The *oikoumenē* was emptied of its temples and filled up with churches, which were not necessarily constructed on the sites of the destroyed temples or with their very stones. Temples, by tradition, were supposed to represent society and so were built on central sites—or at least visible ones like a city's acropolis. The new religion implied another religious geography: it was founded on another conception of the community. Whereas the temples were open, the new churches were closed structures that could be located anywhere. Pagan acts of worship were performed in the open air, the case of Mithraism excepted. Among Christians as among Jews, worship was much less centralized and was practiced inside places of worship. Churches expressed the need for new forms of ritual—simpler, more intimate, where a text was read, sung, commented upon—inside a community that needed to keep to limited dimensions, in order for the voice of the officiating celebrant, reader, or preacher to carry and be heard. The process of Christianization would lead to an increase in sites of worship and a diversity in their locales. For example, in Byzantine Palestine, whereas in the fifth century the church was often built in the center of a town, somewhat replacing the temple, by the sixth century churches were dispersed in various quarters.[3] It is clear this is a new conception of the sta-

2. See Eberhard Sauer, *The Archaeology of Religious Hatred in the Roman and Early Medieval World* (Stroud: Tempus, 2003); and, in particular, Johannes Hahn, *Gewalt und religiöser Konflikt* (Berlin: Akademie Verlag, 2004).

3. See Alan Walmsley, "Byzantine Palestine and Arabia: Urban Prosperity in Late Antiquity," in *Towns in Transition: Urban Evolution in Late Antiquity and the Early Middle Ages*, ed. Neil Christie and Simon T. Loseby (Aldershot, UK: Ashgate, 1996), 126–58.

tus and function of sites of worship in the urban environment, one that is found in other provinces of the empire.

To speak of the appearance of new forms of worship in Late Antiquity rather than of a new spirituality, as E. R. Dodds first did, perhaps allows us to sharpen the analysis of the transformations that religious groups underwent. Such an innovation in divine worship—which deeply horrified the emperor Julian ("I avoid innovation [*kainotomian*] in all things, so to speak, but in particular concerning the gods," he wrote in *Letter* 20, 453b)— could not help but deeply influence relations between religion and political power. It also affected relations between religious communities, since religious identity was now defined, above all, inside a chosen community—even if this community was part of the whole fabric of a dominant religion that had imperial support. I hope to be able to examine here some of the mechanisms of what is well observed in Late Antiquity: the rise in religious intolerance and religious violence—problems that still remain in our heritage, as we know only too well.

Since Fustel de Coulanges's *La cité antique* (1864) and Emile Durkheim's *Les formes élémentaires de la vie religieuse* (1912), we know that civic religion is above all the exteriorized representation of a ritual required of all, or almost all, people in a given society—a ritual supposed to reaffirm collective identity.[4] In the Greco-Roman world, the manifestations of civic religion included public representations of veneration, in designated sites, around prescribed rituals, involving songs, processions, libations, and/or sacrifices. Such manifestations usually ended in festivities and public amusements such as dances, games, or theater.

John Scheid has reflected on the profound transformation of Roman religious practice at the end of the civil wars, especially

4. See, for example, David Porter, *Prophets and Emperors: Human and Divine Authority from Augustus to Theodorus* (Cambridge, MA: Harvard University Press, 1995); Vasiliki Limberis, "'Religion' as the Cipher for Identity: The Cases of the Emperor Julian, Libanius, and Gregory Nazianzus," *Harvard Theological Review* 93 (2000): 373–400.

with Roman expansionism.[5] With the enlargement of the urban community, direct participation by all citizens in worship
became increasingly problematic. Worship became the affair of
representatives of the population. We see how such an evolution would render Roman religion more and more abstract, by
accentuating the distance of the great majority of the population from the cult. Under the empire, the difficulty of developing
a direct religious relationship was accentuated even more, now
bordering on impossibility. Without a change in the nature of
the religion, Scheid tells us, such circumstances would lead to a
certain interiorization of religion: the Roman citizen's religious
participation was now often expressed by reading, that is, in the
intellectual mode. Scheid proposes seeing in this phenomenon
of interiorization, due to the distancing of worship, a *praeparatio
evangelica* of sorts, that would dispose minds to Christianity: in
effect, less civic cult implied a new relation to religion that was
intellectual in nature. Scheid adds that a parallel transformation
is found, already before the destruction of the Jerusalem Temple,
in Diaspora Judaism, a Judaism in which sacrificial worship remains nominal, since it can only be practiced in Jerusalem, and
in which one notes an adherence that is intellectual rather than
concrete to the religion of Israel. I would perhaps hesitate to de-
marcate so clearly between Palestinian Judaism and Diaspora Judaism: such a difference, although traditional, is too convenient
for the orthodoxies, both Christian and Jewish, who insist (each
with inverse vectors of value) on the chiasm between two fundamentally different Judaisms. For Christian theologians, one is
closed and the other open, in Bergsonian terms. For the rabbis,
one is authentic and the other adulterated. The two attitudes
have in common a conception of the Palestinian world as a world

5. John Scheid, "Religione e societa," in *Storia di Roma*, vol. 4, ed. Arnaldo Momigliano, Aldo Schiavone, and Carmine Ampolo (Turin: Giulio Einaudi, 1989), 631–59.
See also John Scheid, *Religion et pieté à Rome* (1985; Paris: La Découverte, 2001), in
particular 119ff.

apart, as if it were not an integral part of the Hellenistic and Roman cultural world. But we know that the development of the synagogue and of Jewish religious communities in the Hellenistic world was found in Palestine as well as in the Diaspora.[6] Scheid's intuition is important, though, and seems to me to run in the direction of my general argument. I would like to propose, along these lines, taking another step by noting that neither distancing nor abstraction would seem to favor a stable and satisfying religious attitude, except among some intellectuals. It is therefore legitimate to postulate that the transformations of religious life discerned by Scheid would quickly become the motor of the formation of new structures for religious communities and the invention of "scriptural communities" of a new kind—whose model, already ancient, was represented by Jewish communities grouped around their synagogues, sites used as much for the hermeneutic study of sacred texts as for worship, *batei midrash* as much as *batei knesset*.[7] It is this communitarianism that will become the natural mode of religion and identity toward the end of Antiquity.

The new care of the self, the rise of religions of the Book, and the end of sacrifices are three aspects (not the only ones, to be sure) of this new religiosity, detectable by a sociopsychological analysis, which seems, *mutatis mutandis*, to cut across the various religious and political identities of Late Antiquity. This new religiosity has both social aspects—such as ritual, the study of the Scriptures, their memorization, and their commentary—and psychological aspects, such as the call to repent in sermons and in asceticism.

The disintegration of the civic model under the empire in the second and third centuries was also true among urban elites who were less and less interested by direct engagement in and

6. See Birget Olsson and Magnus Zetterhold, eds., *The Ancient Synagogue, from Its Origins until 200 CE* (Stockholm: Almqvist and Wiksell, 2003).

7. The idea of "scriptural communities" has been analyzed by Brian Stock, *The Implications of Literacy: Written Languages and Models of Interpretation in the Eleventh and Twelfth Centuries* (Princeton, NJ: Princeton University Press, 1983).

close identification with former values and traditional attitudes. In the fourth century, the civic elite was all too often not really interested in the exercise of its political duties.[8] This disintegration, accompanied by the slow desertion of the classical city, provoked religious choices. Of course this does not mean that religious communities did not exist in the Greco-Roman world. In pages synthesizing the contributions to a rich volume on the subject that was recently edited by Nicole Belayche and Simon Mimouni, John North stresses the capital importance of the evolution of these groups in order to understand the most important changes in the nature of religious life.[9] Using a metaphor borrowed from Peter Berger, North speaks of a "supermarket of religions" in the Roman Empire: people had a choice; people could change religious identity; people converted. The various possibilities were offered to everyone, with a freedom and a richness previously unknown. The freely chosen community was defined by shared belief. Thus, explains North, sacrifice could become over time an act of faith rather than an obligation.

Even if social situations are always integrated into a historical context, they are never without antecedents. Before the third century, the idea of a religious community established on shared beliefs was far from being generalized in the empire. Only a few minorities—certain philosophers, Jews, those "fellow travelers" of Judaism who were the "God-fearers," and Christians—truly

8. See, for example, Clifford Ando, *Imperial Ideology and Provincial Loyalty in the Roman Empire* (Berkeley: University of California Press, 2000), 15; Antigone Samellas, *Death in the Eastern Mediterranean (50–600 A.D.): The Christianization of the East: An Interpretation* (Tübingen: Mohr Siebeck, 2002), 255. For a different perspective, see Claude Lepelley, *Aspects de l'Afrique romaine: Les cités, la vie rurale, le christianisme* (Bari: Edipuglia, 2001).

9. John North, "Réflexions autour des communautés religieuses dans le monde gréco-romain," in *Les Communautés religieuses dans le monde gréco-romain*, ed. Nicole Belayche and Simon Mimouni, Bibliothèque de l'école des hautes études, section des science religieuses, vol. 117 (Turnhout: Brepols, 2003); see also John North, "The Development of Religious Pluralism," in *The Jews among Pagans and Christians in the Roman Empire*, ed. Judith Lieu, John North, and Tessa Rajak (London: Routledge, 1992), 174–93.

represented such religious communities. It was only in the minds of some intellectuals that polytheism could offer the basis of such a community. Even in the *Life of Apollonius of Tyana* by Philostratus, one notes the absence of a community that might be the philosopher's, with which he might identify himself—despite the fact that he evolved in the Pythagorean tradition, a communitarian tradition if ever there was one. The adherence of large sections of society to this type of awareness of self, rather rare until then, was one of the characteristics of the world of Late Antiquity, explains Garth Fowden in a study of these religious communities.[10]

The definition of religion in Rome as the observance of rites, without belief really playing an independent role, seems today finally on its way to being understood and accepted. To understand the radical transformation of religion into a phenomenon that is above all internal—the *vera religio* established over belief with Augustine, for example—we have to notice a significant inversion of the relation between the two pairs of terms: sacred/profane and public/private.[11]

The religion of the Romans, as has been said, was a public affair: "No one shall have gods to himself, either new gods or alien gods, unless recognized by the State," wrote Cicero. Similarly, Marcian: "Sacred things are those that have been consecrated publicly, not in private. If someone in private makes something sacred for himself, this thing is not sacred, but profane."[12]

With the interiorization and subjectivization of religion, the

---

10. Garth Fowden, "Religious Communities," in *Late Antiquity: A Guide to the Post-classical World*, ed. Glen W. Bowersock, Peter Brown, and Oleg Grabar (Cambridge, MA: Harvard University Press, 1999), 82–106. See also Andreas Bendlin, "Gemeinschaft, Öffentlichkeit und Identitat: Forschungberichtliche Anmerkungen zu den Mustern sozialer Ordnung in Rom," in *Religiöse Vereine in der römischen Antike*, ed. Ulrike Egelhaarf-Gaiser and Alfred Schäfer (Tübingen: Mohr Siebeck, 2002), 9–40.

11. On this subject, see the interesting remarks by Daniel Dubuisson, *L'Occident et la religion: Mythes, science et idéologie* (Brussels: Éditions Complexe, 1998), 29ff.

12. Cicero *De legibus* 2.8.19; Marcian *Institutiones* 3: "*Sacrae autem res sunt hae, quae publicae consecratae sunt, non priuatae: si quis ergo priuatim sibi sacrum constituerit, sacrum non est, sed profanum.*" Text cited by Clifford Ando, "Religion and *ius publicum*: Two

two pairs were inverted: in Judaism and Christianity of the early Roman Empire, the field of the sacred was superimposed on that of the private, whereas the public domain became the site of the profane. For Jews as for Christians, the public domain was that of pagan Rome, whereas the true religion—founded on the individual conscience (*conscientia, syneidesis*), even if it was licit (for the Jews)—remained in the private domain (think of the "four cubits of the *halakha*" mentioned in the preceding chapter), since sacrifices were henceforth abolished. For Christians who were still outside the law, this inversion was still more obvious. What was true for Jews and Christians was also true for the many sects that burgeoned in the Near East, between the two poles of monotheism and dualism (the second is the radicalization of the first) and certainly for Manichaeism. Things are never simple, however. If Christianity clearly defined itself as lying outside political frameworks, it found the means in the fourth century to reintegrate them. It is true that depoliticization (*Entpolitisierung*, which for Max Weber represented the attitude of intellectuals left on the margins of power) and re-politicization are two phases in the pendulum swing between religion and politics.[13]

I have referred, in speaking of the rise of the religions of the Book, to the "de-globalization" of the Mediterranean world in Late Antiquity and to the error of Constantine, who believed that Christianity offered him a spiritual basis to unify the empire, whereas the new religion encouraged the centrifugal energies of various cultures. This remark was partly meant to cultivate the paradox, but not only that.[14] Christian emperors tried of course

---

Case Studies," in *Religion and Law in Classical and Christian Rome*, ed. Clifford Ando and Jörg Rüpke (Stuttgart: Steiner, 2006).

13. For a historical analysis of the Weberian concept, see Hans G. Kippenberg, *Die vorderasiatischen Erlösungsreligionen in ihrem Zusammenhang mit der antiken Stadtherr-shaft: Heidelberger Max-Weber-Vorlesungen 1988* (Frankfurt: Suhrkamp, 1991).

14. This is also the starting point of the reflections of Garth Fowden in his *Empire to Commonwealth: Consequences of Monotheism in Late Antiquity* (Princeton, NJ: Princeton University Press, 1993).

to import into Christianity certain aspects of the old civic religion. However, the old model, established upon the public and collective character of religion, had given way to what I propose calling the new model of religion, in which authority is no longer exterior and public, but rather interior or internalized, whether in the self or the sacred Book. In the new model, subjective forms of religion such as faith or piety are dominant, and they model the objective forms that it might take.[15] If religion remained, as formerly, a social (that is to say, collective) fact, in the new circumstances the community was (in principle) chosen by the individual; belonging to the group was based on the conversion of the individual person, or his repenting; and, finally, the reading of Scripture had become a personal duty. All this means that the principle of authority rested largely on the individual. Therefore, the formation of scriptural communities occurs mainly lower down, from below, rather than from above.

What happened with the Christianization of imperial power? Secular power, especially with Justinian, decided to "establish" religion, that is to say, to make orthodox Christianity (the version accepted by the emperor) the focal center of authority. New relations between religion and politics were thus instituted and a new equilibrium established between ecclesiastical and imperial power. This equilibrium was founded, in theory, on the imagined model of biblical Israel: "I have defeated you, O Solomon," exclaimed Justinian upon entering for the first time into Saint Sophia, at least according to legend.[16] The work of Christian emperors, from Constantine to Justinian, could be decoded in more prosaic terms, though: they succeeded in giving Christianity the status and state role that had belonged to civic religion in pa-

---

15. See, for example, Maurice Sachot, *L'Invention du Christ* (Paris: Odile Jacob, 1997), for many judicious remarks on what the author calls "the Christian subversion of Roman religion."

16. On the importance of the Old Testament in Byzantine political theory, see Gilbert Dagron, *Empereur et prêtre: Étude sur le "césaropapisme" byzantin* (Paris: Gallimard, 1996), in particular 68–70; translated into English by Jean Birrell as *Emperor and Priest: The Imperial Office in Byzantium* (Cambridge: Cambridge University Press, 2003).

gan Rome, (but let us not forget) with the difference that Christianity, even as state religion, remained a religion founded on personal decision, repentance, and faith—hence, founded on the idea of the religious community. To give an example of this shift, let us observe what happened among the Jews; as a particular religious minority, the Jews (here as elsewhere) give us a perspective. The Jews retained their legal legitimacy in the Justinian's empire, even if it was now hedged on various sides. But if Judaism remained *religio licita*, this was not true of other religious options. Throughout the medieval times, the Jews would be the only ones to be tolerated in the Christian empire, which did not admit either pagans or heretics or Manichaeans (assimilated in large part to a heretical sect). Similarly, this empire later would not tolerate in any fashion the Muslims, who remained identified as the enemy from outside. The Jews—witnesses of the first revelation, guardians of the sacred books (even if they no longer knew how to read them with the key of truth)—had become a community that was humiliated and despised, certainly, but at least in principle tolerated by imperial power as well as by religious hierarchy.

It seems to me that an argument might be developed that would show that the Muslim concept of *ahl al-dhimma* (as religious communities that could and ought to be tolerated, above all the Jews and Christians, but later on also the Zoroastrians, and even by liberal extension the Hindus, because these communities were founded on prophetic books) finds its distant origins in the status given to Jews by Justinian. The Muslims quite simply would extend it also to Christians, another community that possessed holy Scriptures, which were dethroned by the Qur'an just as the Hebrew Bible had been subsumed by the New Testament.[17]

Whatever the case, it was precisely under Justinian, under the

---

17. See Guy G. Stroumsa, "Religious Dynamics between Christians and Jews in Late Antiquity," in *Cambridge History of Christianity*, vol. 2, *Constantine to c. 600*, ed. Augustine Casiday and Frederick Norris (Cambridge: Cambridge University Press, 2007), 151–72.

very Christian emperor who prided himself on being a theologian, that the Jews of Palestine, for example, defined themselves for the first time in a clear way—and in terms similar, *mutatis mutandis*, to those by which the Christians defined themselves. It was under his reign—while the transformation of the identity of the Holy Land, its intensive Christianization, was being asserted more than ever before—that one can observe the development of the spiritual authority of rabbis over whole communities, a phenomenon that does not seem to have been so clearly asserted beforehand. In other words, Christianization and Judaization went hand in hand, and the marginalization of Jews was also the mark of their identification as a religious community.[18]

The community groupings of Late Antiquity that are not easily discernible at the heart of the Christianized Roman Empire do appear more clearly on its margins, for example, in Mesopotamia. Until the Muslim conquest, this was an immense territory, divided between two imperial powers: the Byzantines on one side and the Sasanians on the other. Both in the towns and in the countryside (*khōra*), one witnesses a veritable mosaic of communities, each with its own religious and cultural identity. J. B. Segal well analyzed this mosaic a long time ago, showing how political power influenced the status of these various communities and the relations among them.[19]

Perhaps the most striking element of these communities is their multiplicity. One finds Christian communities that are very different from each other on both sides of the border, but there are also Jewish and pagan communities, Baptist groups such as the Mandeans, and the Manichaeans.

In an important and complex book that has not received all the attention it deserved, John Wansbrough offered a quarter century ago an unequaled analysis of the essential characteris-

18. This analysis is indebted to Seth Schwartz, *Imperialism and Jewish Society, 200 B.C.E.–640 C.E.* (Princeton, NJ: Princeton University Press, 2001).

19. J. B. Segal, "Mesopotamian Communities from Julian to the Rise of Islam," *Proceedings of the British Academy* (1955): 109–39.

tics of such scriptural communities, proposing to see them as key to the origins of Islam.[20] Wansbrough starts with the hypothesis that it is its capacity to historicize the truth that makes the history of salvation a particular literary type, and also that it is the creation of such a type—and its continuation—that distinguishes the monotheistic confessions from other religious communities. He adds that the organizing principle of a confessional community, its definition of authority, is founded on theological principles rather than on social, economic, or political ones. The Near East of Late Antiquity is characterized, according to him, by the proliferation of such confessional groups, which cannot always be easily distinguished from each other. The means found by these communities to define their identity, by opposing themselves to other communities, is to transform into a ritual the story (the Book) on which they rely. For instance, this is what one observes in early Christianity and in the complex dynamic that will become the struggle between "orthodoxy" and "heresies," or rather that will allow the gradual emergence of orthodoxy—and the censorship, then the suppression, of its competitors. Detailed discussion of the content of revelation, of the holy Book, and its ritual implications thus transforms interconfessional polemic into an essential element of religious identity. For Wansbrough, it is this "sectarian milieu" (which other Arabists prefer to call the "polemical milieu") that was the cradle of nascent Islam. From our perspective here, such a vision of things allows us to integrate into our analysis of the dominant and communitarian forms of religious identity in Late Antiquity a reflection on what has always appeared, at least since Gibbon, as an essential characteristic of this period: the rise in religious violence and intolerance. I would like to proceed to such reflection.

For Gibbon, the victory of Christianity in the Roman Empire was indeed that of the original monotheism of Israel, of a total and totalizing faith, refusing to tolerate the error of idolatry. For

20. John Wansbrough, *The Sectarian Milieu: Contest and Composition of Islamic Salvation History* (1978; repr., Amherst NY: Prometheus Press, 2006).

him, fanaticism and violence in matters of religion derived directly from this characteristic. To that was added, as anti-papist leaven, the Constantinian collusion between religious truth and political power. By the fifth century—let us say after Theodosius II—it is clear that individuals have much less freedom about religion than two centuries previously.[21] Peter Brown here moves against the current in proposing that we not stress violence and intolerance in the process of Christianization.[22] Although the dramatic destructions of temples across the empire (especially in the fifth century) might sometimes hide a more complex and fluid reality and great regional differences, it does seem to a large number of scholars (among whom are Frank Trombley, Ramsey MacMullen, Karl Noetlichs, and Robin Lane Fox, who are opposed by Robert Turcan, among others) that a still lively paganism was brutally destroyed by a militant Christianity.[23] From the valley of the Nile to that of the Rhine, the archaeological remains of Christian iconoclastic violence testify to the angry zeal of the Christians.[24] We know that in Egypt, for example, the success of Christianity was due also to the use of force. They destroyed pagan temples, but they also burned synagogues (even as intellectual a bishop as Ambrose was not scandalized by this) and one cannot exonerate Cyril of Alexandria from the murder of the philosopher Hypatia.[25] Above all, any independent religious thought that was defined as heretical quickly became impossible. At the end of the fourth century, the execution of Priscillian of Avila underlines the collusion of the Church with the "secular

21. See, for example, Robin Lane Fox, *Pagans and Christians* (New York: Knopf, 1987), 23.

22. Peter Brown, *Authority and the Sacred: Aspects of the Christianisation of the Roman World* (Cambridge: Cambridge University Press, 1995), in particular chapter 2, "The Limits of Intolerance," 29–54.

23. See Andreas Bendlin, "Peripheral Centres—Central Peripheries: Religious Communication in the Roman Empire," in *Römische Reichsreligion und Provinzialreligion*, ed. Hubert Cancik and Jörg Rüpke (Tübingen: Mohr Siebeck, 1997), 35–68.

24. See p. 85 n. 2, above.

25. See Maria Dzielska, *Hypatia of Alexandria* (Cambridge, MA: Harvard University Press, 1995), 82–100.

arm"—a collusion that was fated (despite protests) to enjoy such
a long and somber future. It must be recalled that the times were
violent, and there is no need to call upon any theological foundation to explain the violence of religious confrontations. But
the fact remains that the boundaries of freedom of action and
of religious thought were undeniably curtailed in the Christianized empire.

One must pose, once again, the inevitable question of the origins of Christian violence. Was the violence essentially theological, sociological, or ethnic? All these hypotheses have been
proposed, tested, rejected. It is of course impossible for me here
to take up the problem *ab ovo*. Long ago, reflecting on this urgent and permanent problem, I went back to two principal approaches.[26] The first identified the Jewish roots of Christianity,
its monotheism, as the main source of its intolerance. For this
school, crudely speaking that of Gibbon, Christianity had since
its very beginning shown its intolerant character. For the second,
more apologetic school, it was Constantine and Caesaropapism
under its various forms that were the guilty parties. A Christianity without collusion with the state and its power, like that of
the first centuries, was not only historically possible, but even
represented "the true essence of Christianity." In placing these
two options back to back, I had suggested that they both sinned
by historical simplification. A phenomenon as complex as religious violence cannot be explained except over the long duration,
hence by calling upon the dialectic of complex influences and
multiple contexts.

One of the roots of Christian intolerance is no doubt what the
Egyptologist Jan Assmann calls "the Mosaic distinction," that is
to say, the centrality in Hebrew monotheism (unlike the monotheism of Akhenaten, for example) of the idea of truth at the very

26. See Guy G. Stroumsa, "Le radicalisme religieux du premier christianisme: Con-
texte et implications," in *Le Retours aux Écritures: Fondamentalismes présents et passés*, ed.
Evelyne Patlagean and Alain Le Boulluec, Bibliothèque de l'École des hautes études,
section des sciences religeuses, vol. 99 (Louvain: Peeters, 1993), 357–82.

heart of the religion.[27] For the sociologist Rodney Stark, who in-
aptly names this kind of monotheism a "particularism," religious
conflicts were maximized when two or more "particularist" and
strong religious organizations coexisted, rendering theological
disagreement inevitable.[28]

But all that remains quite abstract. That religious communities, since they possess competing versions of the same *historia
sacra*, should be more given to polemic than to tolerance and to
mutual respect is evident. What transformed potentiality into
act, if one can put it like that, is above all the fact that Christians
inherited in the fourth century—without being well prepared
for it (but such preparation is never possible)—Roman imperial
power. In fact, since the birth of Christianity, Christian intellectuals who had remained depoliticized (*entpolitisiert*) felt themselves free to think and write in an "irresponsible" way—regarding everything that dealt with cosmic eschatology at the end of
time, or even about links between political power and the forces
of evil, for example. What would happen when, suddenly after
more than two centuries of exegetical habits, the same intellectuals were obliged to play a politically responsible role, instead
of being content with the apocalyptic? Manifestly, they were not
ready and they continued to think, to write, and to preach as if
the war of the sons of light against the sons of darkness were still
a combat to be won, even when their thinking did not echo triumphalism (as with Eusebius, who had become the mouthpiece
of the Constantinian victory). The lethal mixture, as we see, was
the reuse in a new politicized context of a concept developed
previously in a situation that was so depoliticized that everything
was permitted—for nothing had any consequences. But what

27. See Jan Assmann, *Moses the Egyptian: The Memory of Egypt in Western Monotheism* (Cambridge, MA: Harvard University Press, 1997), 82–100. See further Jan Assmann, *Die Mosaische Unterscheidung, oder der Preis des Monotheismum* (Munich: Carl
Hanser-Verlag, 2003), 19–47.

28. See Rodney Stark, *One True God: Historical Consequences of Monotheism* (Princeton, NJ: Princeton University Press, 2001).

Stark calls "particularism," the conviction of the truth of a religious system (a term that he uses probably because "particularism" is *a priori* pejorative, and he wants to denigrate this kind of system), in fact leads us into error. For what seems to have provoked the slip into active and violent intolerance on the part of the Christianity of Late Antiquity is the combination of a "particularistic" faith with the power of a universal empire. We can see how the term "particularistic" is badly chosen: Christians insisted precisely on offering humanity as a whole their own conception of salvation. In *Civilization and Its Discontents*, Freud writes:

> When once the apostle Paul had posited universal love between men as the foundation of his Christian community, extreme intolerance on the part of Christendom towards those who remained outside it [*die äussertse Intoleranz gegen die draussen Verbliebenen*] became the inevitable consequence. To the Romans, who had not founded their communal life as a State upon love, religious intolerance was something foreign, although with them religion was a concern of the State and the State was permeated by religion.[29]

Even if Freud was not a historian of religions, we know of the strong and constant interest he took in scholarly works dealing with the history of religions and his efforts to keep himself up to date. I have analyzed this text elsewhere and have quoted it here only to remind us that intolerance, like religion, was as much a psychological phenomenon as a sociological one, and psychological reflections cannot be neglected in the study of it.[30]

Like all human groups, the Romans were capable of intolerance when they thought that a religious attitude was putting the integrity of the state in danger, even if the notion of intolerance

29. Sigmund Freud, *Das Unbehagen in der Kultur/Civilization and Its Discontents*, trans. James Strachey (New York: Norton, 1961), 61.

30. See Stroumsa, "Le radicalisme religieux du premier christianisme." On Freud and the history of religions, see Guy G. Stroumsa, "Myth into Novel: The Late Freud on Early Religion," in *New Perspectives on Freud's "Moses and Monotheism,"* ed. Ruth Ginsburg and Ilana Pardes (Tübingen: Niemeyer, 2006), 203–16.

was not a Roman category.[31] On the other hand, Jewish exclusivism (even in the radical forms that it could take in Qumran, for example, where religious hatred was zealously asserted) cannot be compared in its lack of consequences (for the Essenes represented only a minority and marginal community) with the forms of religious intolerance to be observed later in the Christianized Roman Empire.[32]

Christian intolerance was observed first of all in anti-Jewish polemic, which denied that Jews correctly understood their own sacred books. It was only in the fourth century, after the victory against paganism, that this theological anti-Judaism would be transformed into what must be called anti-Semitism: an irrational and total hatred of the Jews, demonized by some Christian authors who applied to them traits reserved until then for the pagans, for example, by describing synagogues as theaters or pagan temples where worship of demons was practiced. John Chrysostum here provides an infamous example, with verbal violence worthy of a Voltaire.[33]

Although the polemic with Judaism was the earliest of Christian polemics, it was not the most violent. In the Roman Empire, Christians were quickly perceived as a threat by the pagan majority. We should not be surprised by the fact that a sect that was still weak, outside the law, and often persecuted could appear to be threatening the very structures of society. As we know too well, collective attitudes are nothing less than irrational. The content of Christian worship, hidden from the public eye and abandoned to the imagination, was considered to be criminal and to in-

31. See, for example, Arnaldo Momigliano, "La religione romana: Il periodo imperiale," in his *Saggi di storia della religione romana*, ed. Riccardo di Donato (Brescia: Morcelliana, 1988), 67–86.

32. Studies of religious intolerance in the Christianized Roman Empire are legion, of course. See in particular H. A. Drake, "Lambs into Lions: Explaining Early Christian Intolerance," *Past and Present* 153 (1996): 3–36. See also Lellia Cracco Ruggini, "Intolerance: Equal and Less Equal in the Roman World," *Classical Philology* 82 (1987): 187–205; and Michael Gaddis, *There Is No Crime for Those Who Have Christ: Religious Violence in the Christian Roman Empire* (Berkeley: University of California Press, 2005).

33. See Stroumsa, *Barbarian Philosophy*, 135–56.

clude human sacrifices, cannibalistic practices, or obscene sexual activities. Christians had beliefs so strange that they were judged to be atheists, an approach encouraged by the refusal of Christians to take part in the public rituals practiced by everyone else.

If the conflict between pagans and Christians is so fascinating, this is primarily due to the stakes of this conflict and its decisive consequences for the future of Western culture. Here I can only stress some aspects to which perhaps not enough attention has been paid. Despite the rivers of ink that they spilled to attack each other, pagans and Christians did not seem to have a great deal to say to each other, as Clifford Ando has noted.[34] One can therefore speak of a disappointing "dialogue of the deaf" between pagan and Christian intellectuals.[35] In many respects, the affair seems to have been a misunderstanding of gigantic proportions. The pagans did not manage to understand that the Christians were proposing a new sort of religion, while the Christians refused to recognize the nature of pagan religion. Under the Roman Empire, in effect, a veritable religious revolution was taking place, a revolution of which the Christians were the principal bearers. This is what explains in large part the final victory of Christianity in the great combat for hearts and minds. It seems to me that the fundamental incomprehension between pagans and Christians about the nature of religion is directly linked to the problem of Christian intolerance. The religious revolution of Late Antiquity was accompanied by radical cultural transformations that introduced ways of thinking and conduct that would later be associated with the Middle Ages, in the East as in the West, in Greek and in Syriac as in Latin. At the core of these transformations we find a great rupture in the parameters of personal and collective identity. Whereas in the Hellenistic world, the question of identity had been primarily posed in cultural terms, by the fifth cen-

34. Clifford Ando, "Pagan Apologetics and Christian Intolerance in the Ages of Themistius and Augustine," *Journal of Early Christian Studies* 4 (1996): 171–207.

35. The expression is that of François Paschoud. See Stroumsa, *Barbarian Philosophy*, 44–56, in particular 44–48.

tury of our era, it had become a question formulated almost solely in religious terms.

In the ancient world, we observe various modes of religious exclusion. The Jews excluded the pagan *ethnoi*, the *goyyim*, who had not shared in divine revelation, while the threshold of tolerance for minority opinion was relatively high in rabbinic literature. For their part, Christians claimed to accept all peoples, but their intellectuals were in general very intolerant of any divergent opinion. But the opposition between a tolerant paganism and an intolerant Christianity is now recognized for what it is: an idealized and stereotyped image. Such an opposition relies in effect on a misinterpretation of the nature of Greek or Roman religion, as Peter Garnsey reminds us.[36]

Origen's *Contra Celsum* remains an inexhaustible treasure for studying the pagan-Christian polemic. Celsus was a Platonist philosopher who wrote his lost treatise *Alēthēs logos* in the 180s, while Origen wrote his refutation of Celsus around the middle of the third century. Their "aborted" dialogue reflects well the basic mutual incomprehension between pagan and Christian intellectuals. Before analyzing the arguments on the two sides, it must be noticed that a parallel between the two positions is deeply biased. Celsus does not represent "paganism" in the same sense that Origen represents Christianity, for the simple reason that a "pagan" entity comparable to Christianity did not exist. Celsus is not a pagan but a philosopher and, as such, one could not call him a "polytheist" either. To a great extent, the Platonists must be considered (and not only them) as monotheists, just like Christian theologians.[37]

The collection of articles recently published by Polymnia Athanassiadi and Michael Frede shows once and for all that there were different sorts of monotheism in Late Antiquity and

36. Peter Garnsey, "Religious Toleration in Classical Antiquity," in *Persecution and Toleration*, ed. W. J. Shiels, Ecclesiastical History Society, no. 21 (Oxford: Blackwell, 1984), 1–27.

37. See p. 101 n. 35, above.

that Christians and Jews were far from possessing a monopoly on this subject.[38] The existence of a pagan monotheism—even if it was different in essence from Jewish or Christian monotheism—highlights the fact that one must look elsewhere for the principal source of the antagonism, and hence for the intolerance, between pagans and Christians.

The great caesura between Celsus and Origen is not located so much around the unity of God as around the nature of religion and its role in the state. Celsus is a conservative who desires to preserve society and its traditional values against an external threat of unknown nature. As such, he remains blind to the spiritual novelty of Christianity that seems to him to undermine the very foundations on which the civil society of the empire is established. For Celsus, religion is above all a matter of cultural tradition. For Origen, it is a matter of truth. While the former is a radical relativist, the latter supports a new form of religion, in a revolutionary sense, established on the "objective" truth of revelation and on personal conviction. Celsus's religion is a central attribute of the state and of society, and is the business of citizens, who try to strengthen social structures. For Origen, it is in the human heart that the true religion is implanted, which calls for revolt against the state of things. Ernst Troeltsch has taught us about the evolution of ancient Christianity, from the eschatological radicalism of the sects to the conservatism of the state religion. Origen is still located before the great shift that would take place two or three generations later. For him, the fact that the kingdom of God is not of this world could only mean great distrust of the ambient political and social system. For Celsus, the structure of the religious world is static, but for Origen, it is dynamic in the extreme. *Contra Celsum* reveals how much the

38. Polymnia Athanassiadi and Michael Frede, eds., *Pagan Monotheism in Late Antiquity* (Oxford: Clarendon Press, 1999). For a critique of certain aspects of this book, see Mark Edwards, "Pagan and Christian Monotheism in the Age of Constantine," in *Approaching Late Antiquity: The Transformation from Early to Late Empire*, ed. Simon Swain and Mark J. Edwards (New York: Oxford University Press, 1999), 211–34. See also James J. O'Donnell, "The Demise of Paganism," *Traditio* 35 (1979): 45–88.

presuppositions of the pagans and Christians were remote from each other, as much about the individual as about society.

What considerably weakened the impact of the intuitions of E. R. Dodds in his classic book on *Pagan and Christian in an Age of Anxiety* is precisely that he did not recognize the various anthropological and sociological implications of the religious ideas in conflict. In a nutshell, the Christians were incapable of understanding the idea of civic religion, and the pagans that of religious truth. Yet the concept of civic religion was exactly one of the great differences, although too rarely recognized as such, between Jews and Christians.[39] As we have seen in discussing sacrifices, they represent the very kernel of any civic religion in the ancient world. The new definition of religious identity by the Christians, in insisting on personal choice and taking a distance from ethnic and cultural identity (starting with that of Israel), prevents Christians from being rooted in a society of the past. As both Jews and pagans noted, the Christian reinterpretation of Judaism remained abstract, and the idea of *verus Israel* remained metaphoric. Jewish exclusivism, which insisted on the clear boundaries of collective identity, remained to a certain extent within the framework of the civic religion of the ancient world (even if it was a separatist civic religion that the Jews were advocating). Such exclusivism, then, with the indifference toward the other that characterizes it, enabled the Jews in the rabbinic era (even when the conditions necessary for civic religion, the conducting of sacrifices, had disappeared) to develop both a certain liberalism of opinion inside the community and tolerance for those remaining outside this community. By contrast, the theological universalism of Christians, as we have seen, had as corollary a dynamic proselytism, as well as intolerance for those who refused to accept the message of love.

39. See Guy G. Stroumsa, "Moses the Lawgiver and the Idea of Civil Religion in Patristic Thought," in *Teologie politiche: Modelli a confronto*, ed. Giovanni Filoramo (Brescia: Morcelliana, 2005), 135–48.

Among the pagan intellectuals under the empire, one could certainly find a tradition of tolerance for divergent opinions and attitudes. Porphyry, once again, is a good example, he who in *On Abstinence* stressed tolerance toward various attitudes. Until the peace of the Church, however, it was especially among Christian writers that one finds a sustained defense of the idea of religious tolerance: in fact, it was the Christians (not the pagans) who had urgent need of tolerance at the time. At the turn of the third century, for example, a mind as pugnacious as Tertullian's was capable of developing a long argument in favor of religious tolerance.[40] In the fourth century, though, it was the turn of pagan thinkers, now on the defensive, to produce defenses and illustrations of religious tolerance. Here the great names in the second half of the fourth century are Libanius (the great rhetor of Antioch, admirer of Julian but respected by Theodosius), Themistius (both a philosopher and tutor to Arcadius, son of Theodosius), and the orator Symmachus (a ferocious enemy of Christianity who attacked Gratian for having abolished the traditional cult, during the affair of the altar to Victory in Rome in 382).[41] It was in his plea in favor of dissident attitudes that Symmachus wrote the famous sentence: "*Non uno itinere perveniri potest ad tam grande secretum*" (Such a great secret is not attainable by a single path).[42] Themistius pleaded for religious tolerance before the emperors Valentinian and Valens, with the argument that "the glory of God grows by knowledge, [and] religious differences are only the consequence of His unattainable majesty and

40. See Guy G. Stroumsa, "Tertullian on Idolatry and the Limits of Tolerance," in *Tolerance and Intolerance in Early Judaism and Christianity*, ed. Graham N. Stanton and Guy G. Stroumsa (Cambridge: Cambridge University Press, 1998), 173–84.

41. See, for example, A. H. Armstrong, "The Way and the Ways: Religious Tolerance and Intolerance in the Fourth Century A.D.," *Vigiliae Christianae* 38 (1984): 1–17; Paolo Frezza, "L'esperienza della tolleranza religiosa fra pagani e cristiani dal IV al V sec. d. c. nell'oriente ellenistico," *Studia et Documenti Historiae Iuris* 55 (1989): 41–97.

42. Symmachus *Relatio* 3.10. See Brian Crocke and Jill Harries, *Religious Conflict in Fourth-Century Rome: A Documentary Study* (Sydney: Sydney University Press, 1982), 37–38.

human limitations." For Themistius, culture and faith were two different things, and piety ought to be left to free choice.[43] In this he opposed Julian, who like Celsus saw in the pluralism of national cults a response to the claims by Christians.[44] The attitudes of pagan intellectuals in the fourth century were marked by the religious revolution embarked upon by Constantine. While the passionate arguments that most of them devoted to tolerance were manifestly sincere, it does seem that Julian's intolerance echoes a strong Christian influence.[45]

In the 340s, Firmicus Maternus had been the first Christian writer to ask explicitly for a "zero degree of tolerance" toward pagan worship.[46] Pagan gods were not true gods, and the false worship rendered to them did induce error. Such an attitude was founded on the new definition of religion promoted by Christians: religion was now identical to the truth, in opposition to a whole tradition at least since Varro, which distinguished clearly between religion and truth. It is this transformation of the very idea of religion that is the foundation of the opposition between *vera* and *falsa religio*—an opposition transferred into the language of the law by Valens, Gratian, and Valentinian, and developed by Augustine.[47]

On the other hand, the new definition of religion signified that *superstitio*, now made equivalent to idolatry, should be categorically condemned. Starting from different points of view, Michele

43. On Themistius, see John Vanderspoel, *Themistius and the Imperial Court: Oratory, Civic Duty, and Paideia from Constantius to Theodosius* (Ann Arbor: University of Michigan Press, 1995).

44. See Gilbert Dagron, "L'Empire romain d'Orient au IVᵉ siècle et les traditions politiques de l'hellénisme: Le témoignage de Thémistios," *Travaux et Mémoires* 3 (Paris, 1968), in particular 149–86.

45. See, for example, Glen W. Bowersock, *Julian the Apostate* (Cambridge, MA: Harvard University Press, 1978).

46. See the introduction by Robert Turcan to his edition of *Firmicus Maternus: L'erreur des religions païennes* (Paris: Belles Lettres, 1982), in particular 28–49.

47. See B. Kötting, *Religionsfreiheit und Toleranz im Altertum*, Rheinisch-Westfälische Akademie der Wissenschaften, G 223 (Opladen: Westdeutscher Verlag, 1977).

Salzman and Maurice Sachot have both shown how the pair *religio/superstitio* was semantically inverted by patristic authors.[48]

In the Hellenistic world and in the pagan Roman Empire, identity had been especially defined in cultural terms, particularly linguistic ones. From both the new definition of religion founded on personal faith and the new conception of identity that stressed religion much more than previously would be born what is now called the "new religiosity" of Late Antiquity.

For the polymath Varro in the first century BCE, the *theologia civilis* represented the public dimension of religious rituals. For the first Christians, adherents of a *religio illicita*, there was obviously no question of a public dimension to their faith. The collective space of religion was for them the community of believers, a community without any political dimension. As we have seen, religious communities had existed for a long time in the empire, but they were in free competition on an open market. Only the Christians insisted on total adherence.

The shift from civic religion to communitarian religion was neither radical nor total, of course. But the new accent placed on community underscored the transformation over a few decades (from 312 to 392) of the status of the *religio illicita* into first a religion that became permitted, then official, and finally turned into the sole legal religion of the empire. Christians were finally confronted with the political dimensions of their religion, whose universalism obliged them to go beyond the limits of the empire. Unlike Islam, for which the political dimension of the *umma* of believers was essential from its beginnings, Christianity never succeeded in overcoming the deep ambivalence vis-à-vis the political sphere that had been its birthmark.

Since Hegel at least, Christianity has been conceived of as a powerful effort at interiorizing religious attitudes, those of the

48. Michele R. Salzman, "The Evidence from the Conversion of the Roman Empire to Christianity in Book 16 of the Theodosian Code," *Historia* 42 (1993): 362–78; Maurice Sachot, "*Religio/Superstitio*: Historique d'une subversion et d'un retournement," *Revue de l'Histoire des Religions* 208 (1991): 355–94.

Jews as well as of the pagans: internalizing of worship with the weakening or disappearance of the idea of ritual purity, and internalizing of belief with the all-powerfulness of faith. Internalization in such a context equals spiritualization (a process of universal dimensions, which would only be accomplished at the Stift of Tübingen). Obviously, spiritualization is being conceived *in bonam partem*: it is presumed that the more a religion is internalized, the more it is spiritualized, and the less it is intolerant. Such an assertion is founded on nothing other than the assurance that Westerners too often have of their religious, cultural, and ethical superiority. But one has only to recall the example of Augustine, the great discoverer of the interior man, but also one of the very first to propose collusion between ecclesiastical power and secular power to break religious dissidence by force, in order to realize that the two currents are not totally independent of each other in his thinking.

The world of Late Antiquity was therefore a new axial time, or *Achsenzeit*, no less crucial for the future than the one identified by Karl Jaspers around the middle of the first millennium before our era. It was a world of transformations: political transformations first of all, with the reforms of Diocletian, and then those of Constantine, which marked the end of the ancient city and the centralization of the monarchy. Social transformations, too, with the elites abandoning their towns for Constantinople, where power and honors were concentrated, and the development of a strictly hierarchical society. All these transformations, long since identified as such, have been well studied in their various aspects.[49] Here I have sought to address a third series of transformations, religious in essence. In dealing respectively with what I have called a "new care of the self," the rise of the religions of the Book, the end of sacrifices, and the shift from civic religion to communitarian religion, I have tried to show that some of the major anthropological, cultural, and political transforma-

49. See Suzanne Saïd, Monique Trédé, and Alain Le Boulluec, *Histoire de la littérature grecque* (Paris: Presses Universitaires de France, 1997), 529ff.

tions of Late Antiquity can only be understood as directly linked to certain far-reaching changes in the very concept of religion. Thus alongside the "theologico-political" and the perennial problem of links between religious authority and political authority, one might perhaps speak of the "theologico-anthropological," which points to the dialectical contacts between conceptions of the divine world and concepts of the human person, and also of the "theologico-cultural," where reciprocal relations between religious conceptions and cultural evolution are foregrounded. In all these various aspects, we see why one can never speak of "religion in a pure state" or of cultural phenomena without intimate ties to religion. We have seen how the end of public sacrifices allowed the crystallization of new forms of ritual, yet without managing to totally suppress the very idea of blood sacrifice (animal and sometimes even human). Nor does the reinterpretation of ritual remain in the single register of the religious, either: sacrifice suppressed and reinterpreted, in effect, touches both the "theologico-anthropological" and the "theologico-political."

5

From Wisdom Teacher to Spiritual Master

When the great rhetorician Libanius was asked on his deathbed which one of his disciples should be considered as his successor, he answered: "John would have been my successor, had the Christians not snatched him." This vignette alludes to the conversion of John of Antioch, "the most holy John," as Theodoretus calls him, a disciple of Libanius who had also studied with the philosopher Andragathius. Born into a noble family, John had planned to become a lawyer. After his conversion, however, he abandoned his previous plans and persuaded his disciples Theodore of Mopsuestia and Maximus of Seleucia to renounce the active life and to choose the life of simplicity. The story of this conversion, as summarized by Sozomenus, shows to what extent, toward the end of the fourth century, the passage from pagan wisdom to Christian spirituality was both possible and easy.[1]

---

1. Sozomenus, *H.E.* 8.2 (*P.G.* 67.1513b ff.); Theodoretus, *H.E.* 5.40 (347.18ff. Parmentier); Socrates, *H.E.* 6.3 (*P.G.* 67.665a–668a). These texts are analyzed by A. J. Festugière, *Antioche païenne et chrétienne: Libanius, Chrysostome et les moines de Syrie*, Bibliothèque des écoles françaises d'Athènes et de Rome, no. 194 (Paris: E. de Boccard, 1959), 181. I wish to thank Brouria Bitton-Ashkelony for reminding me of Festugière's book and for her remarks on a previous version of this text.

I have purposely juxtaposed, somewhat schematically, pagan wisdom and Christian spirituality. The life of thought and spirit is infinitely complex, and of course one can also recognize *pagan* spirituality and *Christian* wisdom. My intention here, however, is to underline mainly the vectors, the main trends. The issue at hand is a rather understudied aspect of the Christianization of the elites in the Roman Empire and its anthropological consequences. Identity, which in the Hellenistic world had been defined primarily in cultural and linguistic terms, became essentially religious in the Roman Empire. This change amounted to nothing less than a revolution in the criteria of identity. This revolution was also reflected in the educational patterns of elites, in the modes of transmission of knowledge and of intellectual and spiritual power. The Christian elites knew, perhaps better than others, how to adapt to the cultural frameworks of the Roman Empire, and they adapted these frameworks to their spiritual demands and needs, in particular to their own educational traditions. In the Christianized empire, the education of the traditional elites (both the cultural and the social elites) would remain more or less identical to what it had been in the pagan empire. The clearer and most drastic change occurred within the new, purely Christian monastic movement, which radically broke away from the traditional forms of elite education. A complete picture of the new forms of spiritual formation in early Christianity remains beyond the scope of this presentation, which will be limited to some expressions of the monastic movement and will not deal with the Christian *Didascalia* or with theological schools such as the one in Alexandria.

Although "spiritual direction" is a modern concept, invented by post-Tridentine Catholicism,[2] it is legitimately used to describe a phenomenon already present in the formative period of Christianity in the Roman Empire. The term may be modern, but not the phenomenon. Spiritual direction represents a central aspect

---

2. See, for instance, J.-P. Schaller, "Direction spirituelle," in *Dictionnaire critique de théologie*, ed. Jean-Yves Lacoste (Paris: Presses Universitaires de France, 1998), 336–38.

of religious practice in Late Antiquity, from Roman and Constantinopolitan aristocratic society to the monks of the Egyptian desert. No less important than the existence of the phenomenon itself, however, is the fact that this spiritual direction is expressed rather differently in various cultural and religious milieus: among cultural elites and in humbler social strata, in cities and in the desert, among pagans and Christians. We thus find a series of different attitudes, which express various aspects of spiritual direction in Late Antiquity.[3] Conversion, the shift from philosophy to monasticism (which was defined by its early theoreticians as "true philosophy"),[4] entails some significant transformations of the person. These transformations reflect the radical character of the Christian revolution.

Without denying the evident elements of continuity between Greco-Roman and early Christian thought, we must recognize a major discontinuity in the very concept of person, which is closely related to some fundamental traits of Christian theology. I have sought elsewhere to analyze these traits. They are linked to the implications, direct and indirect, of the relationship between body and soul in a religion that insisted, like Judaism, upon the unity of man, created by God as the conjunction of soul and body, in the expectation of the resurrection of the body. The incarnation of Jesus Christ, however, adds power and urgency to this anthropology. Manifestly, such an anthropology went against various current or acceptable Greek conceptions (in particular the Platonic ones), according to which the human being was, first of all, the human soul or mind.[5]

3. See J. Hevelone Harper, "Spiritual Direction," in *Late Antiquity: A Guide to the Postclassical World*, ed. Glen W. Bowersock, Peter Brown, and Oleg Grabar (Cambridge, MA: Harvard University Press, 1999), 704–5.

4. See Anne-Marie Malingrey, *"Philosophia": Étude d'un groupe de mots dans la littérature grecque, des présocratiques au IVe siècle après J.-C.* (Paris: Klincksieck, 1961).

5. See Guy G. Stroumsa, *Barbarian Philosophy: The Religious Revolution of Early Christianity*, Wissenschaftliche Untersuchungen zum Neuen Testament, no. 112 (Tübingen: Mohr Siebeck 1999), chap. 8. The transformation of ethics represents another aspect of what I have called the religious revolution of early Christianity. On this topic,

Here I shall approach this transformation from the particular angle of spiritual direction. My intention is to examine the conditions under which spiritual direction was possible and what it meant. I shall try, in particular, to identify the differences in the relationship between teacher and disciple among pagans and Christians. Oddly enough, such a comparison does not seem to have been attempted until now.

Arnaldo Momigliano once noted that "the type of priest who is also a spiritual director and a confessor remains almost unknown in Greece and in Rome until the oriental religions come to replace the old cults. . . . A part-time priest," he added, "is not likely to become an effective spiritual guide."[6] Momigliano's remark is only half true, and it puts us on the wrong track, it seems to me, by suggesting we look for the origins of spiritual direction in a "full-time priesthood." Spiritual direction in the ancient world is not related to priesthood. The spiritual teacher is by nature opposed to the priest. For whereas the priest is a religious functionary in charge of daily worship, he does not care for restless souls and does not help them, intensely and individually, in their search for salvation.

As there was no such thing as "pagan spiritual leadership" in Antiquity, it is probably in the direction of prophecy that one should look for the origin of spiritual direction. In ancient Israel, it is the prophet (and the apocalyptic writer under the Second Temple) who appeals to the individual and insists on the demands of personal responsibility, ethical as well as religious. A

---

see Paul Veyne, "Païens et chrétiens devant la gladiature," *Mélanges de l'École française de Rome (Mémorial Charles Pietri)* III, no. 2 (Rome, 1999): 893–917. Veyne insists on the decisive newness of the Christian ethics of interiority.

6. Arnaldo Momigliano, "Seneca between Political and Contemplative Life," in *Quarto contributo alla storia degli studi classici e del mondo antico* (1950), Storia e letteratura, no. 115 (Rome: Edizioni di storia e letteratura, 1969), 239–65. See also Guy G. Stroumsa, "Arnaldo Momigliano and the History of Religions," in *Momigliano and Antiquarianism: Foundations of the Modern Cultural Sciences*, ed. Peter N. Miller (Toronto: University of Toronto Press, 2007).

Talmudic passage seems to corroborate this view.[7] The rabbis discuss the respective merits of the prophet and the sage. The prophet is the hero of a time-hallowed tradition, as reflected in the biblical books. For the rabbis, however, the gates of prophecy have been closed for a long time. The sage, on the other hand, represents the urgent intellectual and spiritual needs of the present. The rabbis thus conclude that the sage is superior to the prophet (*ḥakham ʿadif mi-navi*): this represents a victory of the moderns over the ancients—too rare in Judaism, as elsewhere. Note that the priest is not seriously considered in this context, as his role has become merely symbolic. After the destruction of the Temple, indeed, the priest had no function. But even prior to that destruction, his role remained limited to Temple worship. It is the sages, successors of the prophets, who become the exempla of elitism.[8]

Scholars of spiritual direction (or what the Germans call *Seelenführung*) in the ancient world, and in particular in the Roman world, have sought to compare philosophical and patristic or monastic texts.[9] Oddly enough, the role of the Talmudic sage and his relationship with his best students (the *talmidei ḥakhamim*) has not been compared either to that of the abbot, or *gerōn*, or to

7. Babylonian Talmud, *Baba Batra* 12a.

8. See Ephraim Elimelech Urbach, *The Sages: Their Concepts and Beliefs* (Hebrew ed. 1969; Jerusalem: Magnes Press, 1975), chap. 16; see also Urbach, "Status and Leadership in the World of the Palestinian Sages" (in Hebrew), in *Proceedings of the Israel Academy of Sciences and Humanities* 2 (1968). On rabbinic attitudes toward prophecy, see Urbach, "When Did Prophecy End?" (in Hebrew), *Tarbiz* 17 (1946): 1–11.

9. See in particular Pierre Hadot, "Exercices spirituels antiques et ʿphilosophie chrétienne,ʾ" in *Exercices spirituels et philosophie antique* (Paris: Études augustiniennes, 1981). Hadot points out that what for the philosophers was an ethical exercise becomes with the Christians a spiritual exercise (60), adding that the ideas of penance and obedience totally transform the philosophical practice of spiritual direction (73–74). See further Pierre Hadot, "The Spiritual Guide," in *Classical Mediterranean Spirituality: Egyptian, Greek, Roman*, ed. A. H. Armstrong (New York: Routledge and Kegan Paul, 1986), 436–59, which treats the problem in the *longue durée*, throughout Antiquity. For the philosophical tradition, see mainly I. Hadot, *Seneca und die griechisch-römische Tradition der Seelenleitung*, Quellen und Studien zur Geschichte der Philosophie, no. 13 (Berlin: De Gruyter, 1969); and, before her, Paul Rabbow, *Seelenführung: Methodik der Exerziten in der Antike* (Munich: Kösel-Verlag, 1954) (*non vidi*).

that of the philosopher.[10] One wonders at this strange absence of the Talmudic sage in the comparative history of the formation of elites in the Roman world.[11] It is after all in synagogues, and not in philosophical schools, that Jesus and Paul preached, and it is around the *beit ha-midrash* that they had received their education.[12] To be sure, the Talmudic sage is not the exact equivalent of the monastic spiritual guide. Nevertheless, even a superficial analysis of the sage's role and methods would easily detect numerous and significant parallels with those of both the philosopher and the *higumen*. Side by side with his properly didactic role, the Talmudic sage is also a spiritual teacher. Or rather, for the rabbi (the Talmudic sage), just as for the philosopher (the Hellenic sage), the path of wisdom is also a spiritual path. Within the framework of rabbinic education, way of life and patterns of teaching are as intertwined as they are in the philosophical schools. Indeed, Elias Bickerman once suggested we see the Talmudic schools of thought as an imitation of the various Greek philosophical schools.[13] In a sense, the rabbi's role appears to be a combination of the didactics of the pagan teacher and the spiritual guidance of the Christian teacher. Like the latter, the rabbi sees his role as caring for the formation of those whom Max Weber called "religious virtuosi." One should note, however, the complexity of the picture in Israel in the first century of our era.

10. See Elias J. Bickerman, "The Historical Foundations of Post-Biblical Judaism," in *The Jews, Their History*, ed. Louis Finkelstein, 4th ed. (New York: Schocken, 1970), 111: "Post-Maccabean Judaism adopted the most important idea of Hellenism, that of *paideia*, of perfection through liberal education."

11. See, for instance, the entries on "Direction spirituelle" in *Dictionnaire de Spiritualité*, vol. 3, 1003ff., where much attention is given to the phenomenon in Greece and in Rome, but in which Judaism is wholly absent.

12. On this topic, see the remarks of K. H. Rengstorf, "*Didaskô, ktl.*," in *Theological Dictionary of the New Testament*, ed. Gerhard Kittel; trans. and ed. Geoffrey Bromiley (Grand Rapids, MI: Eerdmans, 1964–76), 2:135–65, on the Hellenistic origins of the concept of *rav* in that of *didaskalos*.

13. See n. 11 above. One may consider the relationship between master and disciple in Judaism as reflecting the direct influence of Greek models. See, for instance, K. H. Rengstorf, "*Manthanô, ktl.*," in *Theological Dictionary of the New Testament*, ed. Kittel, 4:390–461, esp. 439.

From Qumran to the Pharisees, among priests, scribes, and magicians, solutions to the relationship between teacher and disciple varied greatly.

The following pages adopt the task of outlining, at least roughly, a comparative phenomenological analysis of the relationship between guide and disciple among pagan philosophers and the Christian "new philosophers," the monks.[14] In other words, I shall seek to describe the transformation of one kind of personal authority and elite formation into another. Phenomenological analysis, which emphasizes the major trends, must avoid simplistic taxonomies. Let me insist on the fact that the various intellectual and charismatic elements are probably to be found among all the different groups. What distinguishes elite formation among Jews, pagans, and Christians is mainly the relative weight of intellectual and soteriological tendencies within the internal equilibrium of the system.

In early Christianity, one should underline the aspect of rupture with the past, rather than that of continuity. This is true regarding the transmission of both cultural traditions and religious ideals. The paramount importance of charisma and the weakening of intellectual tradition among the disciples of Jesus represent notable landmarks here. So are the Pauline Epistles, which preach a revolt against ideas of knowledge and wisdom as they were understood by both the Pharisaic teaching of Paul's youth and contemporary Greco-Roman philosophical *koinē*. It is within such a perspective that one can first discern the roots of subsequent Christian spiritual direction. Only at the end of the second century would the idea of a school of thought similar to the Greek philosophical schools, at least in its fundamental structures,

14. For a comparative study of spiritual direction among pagans and Christians in the third century, see Richard Valantasis, *Spiritual Guides of the Third Century: A Semiotic Study of the Guide-Disciple Relationship in Christianity, Neoplatonism, Hermetism, and Gnosticism* (Minneapolis: Fortress Press, 1991). Valantasis mainly studies four texts: the "Speech of Thanks to Origen" by Gregory the Wonder-Maker, Porphyry's *Life of Plotinus*, and two texts from Nag Hammadi, *On the Eighth and the Ninth* and *Allogenes*.

appear among some Christian intellectuals (in particular Clement of Alexandria and Origen). This would lead in the third and fourth centuries to the rise of two competing models of religious virtuosity: on the one hand, the Gnostic model, with its ideal of contemplation, of *theiōsis*; on the other hand, the holy man, the ideal of *askēsis*, of *imitatio Christi*. To be sure, these two models do not oppose one another in a radical fashion. The patristic authors even often tell us that one leads to the other, that one can reach saving knowledge (*gnōsis*) only through faith (*pistis*). Nonetheless, we can clearly identify here two distinct intentions, two different vectors.

Spiritual direction, as it is found among the desert monks from the fourth century on, bears only a vague resemblance to the role of the theologian-teacher in third-century Alexandria or Ceasarea. The whole didactic and intellectual element that was so central in the Christian "schools" seems to have disappeared from early monastic literature. Following the Jews, the Christians had picked up the Greek idea of *paideia*—and had transformed it.[15] Among the monks, wisdom is found only in a metaphorical, weak sense. It is not even identical with the new Christian wisdom, which the Church fathers call "true gnosis" (in contradistinction to the false gnosis of the heretics), and whose strong soteriological character immediately differentiates it from both Jewish and Greek wisdom.

It is tempting to see the growth of the spiritual element in the teacher-disciple relation among the Christians as related to the shrinking of the intellectual dimension. It is perhaps more helpful, however, to stress the direction in which the education of the new Christian elites is evolving. Spiritual direction appears most clearly where personal charisma is most important, and where the intellectual element remains limited. The idea of spiritual

15. See Henri I. Marrou, *The History of Education in Antiquity* (1948; repr., Madison: University of Wisconsin Press, 1986), part 3, chap. 9: "Christianity and Classical Education." See also Werner Jaeger, *Early Christianity and Greek Paideia* (Cambridge, MA: Harvard University Press, 1961).

direction grows precisely with the weakening of the intellectual dimension in teaching, and as the power of the individual (at least the elite individual) to find within himself, and by himself, the way to his personal salvation is diminishing. One sees, then, how much spiritual direction reflects a deep transformation of ancient culture.

In order to better understand the Christian novelty, let us first observe some aspects of the teaching of Greek wisdom that were common to the various philosophical schools. The philosopher (the "pagan" sage) may not be a real spiritual master, in the Christian sense of the word. Nevertheless, the "master of wisdom" is a traditional and well-established figure in the Roman world, a sage standing in front of a few disciples, to whom he offers an oral teaching based upon a series of texts.

The search for the origins of the idea of spiritual direction in the Greek philosophical tradition should go back to the great formative period, from the seventh to the fourth centuries BCE. Socrates is of course the main figure of reference. He is the first to have established dialogue, and hence personal and privileged relations between teacher and disciple, as the foundation of any teaching of wisdom. But it is mainly in the leading Hellenistic philosophical schools that the teacher's authority would grow. Let us consider, for instance, Epicurus, who is referred to explicitly as *hēgemōn* (guide) in the writings emanating from his teaching, for instance in his third letter, the *Letter to Menoeceus*.

The complex transformation of philosophy under the empire deeply modified teaching in the various schools. Doctrines and methods mixed, in particular among the Stoics and the Platonists, who established themselves as the two leading schools. This transformation dramatically emphasized the soteriological dimension of philosophy. Particularly from the third century on, under growing Christian influence, to become the disciple of a philosopher increasingly meant to confide oneself to him in order to find the way to personal salvation.

As A. D. Nock showed in his seminal study on conversion, one speaks in Antiquity about conversion to philosophy as one speaks of religious conversion. This conversion entails not only the acceptance of new doctrines, but also adopting a strictly structured way of life, including alimentary and clothing rules, and the submission to a master.[16] The transformation of philosophy will be finally accomplished with Proclus, for whom the *Chaldean Oracles*, that strange blend of high-flown verbosity, would become the staple philosophical diet, on a par with Plato. Epictetus and Marcus Aurelius represent key moments in this history, but I have chosen Seneca here to illustrate our theme. Seneca is contemporaneous with Paul—we even possess an interesting apocryphal correspondence between them.[17] Christian writers would refer to "*Seneca saepe noster*," thus revealing a certain "family resemblance" between the tone of his writing and that of their own, at least as regards anthropology and ethics.

The Stoic sage, as he appears in Seneca's writings (especially in his admirable *Letters to Lucilius*), does not shun the ordinary mortals from whom he differs drastically. On the contrary, he agrees to appear in public, although he does not make an exhibition of himself: "*Id age, ut otium tuum non emineat, sed appareat*" ([Act so] that your retirement be not conspicuous, though it should be obvious).[18] As Paul Veyne writes in his brilliant introduction to Seneca's prose writings, the Stoic sage is a "man-doctrine."[19] It is with formulas from religious language that Seneca describes the sage; he shows the way toward *securitas*, toward wisdom. This permits him to neutralize troubling passions (*apatheia*) and to reach

16. Arthur Darby Nock, *Conversion: The Old and the New in Religion from Alexander the Great to Augustine of Hippo* (1933; repr., Lanham, MD: University Press of America, 1988).

17. See L. Bocciolini Palagi, *Epistolario apocrifo di Seneca e San Paolo* (Florence: Biblioteca Patristica, 1985).

18. Seneca *Letter to Lucilius* 1.19.2; English translation by Richard Gummere, Loeb Classical Library, vol. 1 (London: Heinemann, 1917).

19. Paul Veyne, ed., *Sénèque, Entretiens: Lettres à Lucilius* (Paris: Laffont, 1993), 591. See also H. Cancik-Lindemaier, "Seneca's Collection of Epistles: A Medium of Philosophical Communication," in *Ancient and Modern Perspectives on the Bible and Culture: Essays in Honor of Hans Dieter Betz*, ed. Adela Yarbro Collins (Atlanta: Scholars Press, 1998), 88–109. This article stresses pedagogy aiming at progress toward virtue.

total peace of the soul, in the face of the passions and storms of the world (*hēsychia*, which will become one of the main goals of the Christian monk).[20] The true Stoic sage transforms himself in a radical way, enacting a real transfiguration, rather than achieving some moral or intellectual progress: "*Intellego, Lucili, non emendari me tantum sed transfigurari*" (I really feel, my dear Lucilius, that I am being not only reformed but transformed).[21] He thus reaches a real divinization: "*Des opportet illi divinum aliquid, caeleste, magnificum*" (You must grant that the wise man has an element of godliness, heavenliness, grandeur).[22] He becomes, as it were, a heavenly figure similar, *mutatis mutandis*, to the Confucian sage, as pointed out by Veyne.[23] One may perhaps detect here the trace of the strong influence exerted by neo-Pythagoreanism upon Seneca (hence his vegetarianism). In the Pythagorean tradition, Pythagoras, the very exemplum of the sage, was in intimate contact with divinity.[24]

Such a sage has no need of any kind of spiritual guidance. What he does need is the presence of another sage, with whom he may discuss and reflect.[25] Practically speaking, meeting such a sage is very rare, as Seneca knows well.[26] Lucilius, Seneca himself, and all of us can only hope in our weakness to reach the status of disciples of wisdom. We thus need to put our trust in a mas-

20. Seneca *Letter to Lucilius* 5.51.3. "Some have reached virtue without anybody's help; they found their way themselves (*fecisse sibi ipsos viam*)." Epicurus, Fragment 192. For *securitas*, see Veyne, introduction to *Sénèque, Entretiens*, xlv.

21. Seneca *Letter to Lucilius* 6.1.

22. Ibid., 9.87.19.

23. See also H. Cancik and H. Cancik-Lindemaier, "Seneca's Konstruktion des Weisen: Zur Sakralisierung der Rolle des Weisen im 1. Jh. n. Chr.," in *Weisheit*, ed. Aleida Assmann, Archäologie der literarischen Kommunikation, no. 3 (Munich: W. Fink Verlag, 1991), 205–22.

24. Thus does Iamblichus, in particular, represent him in his *Life of Pythagoras*. See Iamblichus, *On the Pythagorean Way of Life*, ed. and trans. John M. Dillon and Jackson P. Hershbell (Atlanta: Scholars Press, 1991), 2.

25. Seneca *Letter to Lucilius* 18.109.

26. Similarly, Porphyry will note in his *Vita Plotini* (chap. 23) that his teacher had reached the mystical experience of unification with the divine only four times in his life.

ter of wisdom, who will show us the way to follow, through his teaching, but also through his example.[27] "In the meantime, on practical matters, the path should be pointed out for the benefit of one who is still short of perfection, but is making progress."[28] "The soul should accordingly be guided at the very moment when it is becoming able to guide itself. Boys study according to direction."[29] Pierre Hadot insists that the real question here is not *what* one talks about, but *who* talks. The Stoic teacher of wisdom appears to his closest disciples as a true model, a living exemplum, with all the power of this term in the Christian intellectual tradition.[30] One can observe the same phenomenon among the neo-Pythagoreans, as reflected, for instance, in Porphyry's *Life of Pythagoras* and, even more, in the one written by Iamblichus.[31]

But who are his disciples? What is this elite that he is entrusted with forming? Up to late Neoplatonism, the philosophical schools do not really have fixed structures. It is less a matter of buildings and institutions than of persons. If the master disappears, everything collapses. It is the relationship between master and student that creates the school, through teaching and learning, modeling and following.[32] But this teaching, the observation of this example, is not free of charge. Hence the students of wisdom are those whose parents can afford such an education. Intellectual and spiritual elites are recruited in the privileged socio-

27. Seneca *Letter to Lucilius* 94.50. The sage is helpful to those who lack self-confidence: "We are indeed uplifted merely by meeting wise men; and one can be helped by a great man even when he is silent" (94.40).

28. Ibid., 15.50.

29. Ibid., 15.51.

30. See Peter Brown, "The Saint as Exemplar in Late Antiquity," *Representations* 1 (1983): 1–25.

31. Rather than a life of Pythagoras, this last text presents in effect a model of Pythagorean lifestyle. See, for instance, Dillon and Hershbell's introduction to Iamblichus, *On the Pythagorean Way of Life*, and Luc Brisson and A. Ph. Segonds, *Jamblique, Vie de Pythagore* (Paris: Les Belles Lettres, 1996).

32. See Garth Fowden, "The Platonist Philosopher and His Circle in Late Antiquity," *Philosophia* 7 (1977): 359–83, who points out that the disciples tended not to maintain the group identity after the master's death; see also J. Bidez, "Le philosophe Jamblique et son école," *Revue des Études Grecques* 32 (1919): 29–40.

economic classes, that is, only within the urban elites. This sociological phenomenon points to one of the essential differences
with regard to education between the Hellenic tradition and
among both Jews and Christians.

In the ancient world, spiritual direction was thus inscribed in
a preexisting social network: urban elites.[33] While Christian intellectuals and teachers, from the second century onward, do not
disdain to proselytize among these elites, in Alexandria, Rome, or
elsewhere, these elites are in no way the single or privileged field
of their efforts. Christian propaganda reflects the tension, noted
long ago by Ernst Troeltsch, between two opposite tendencies,
between the desires for cultural continuity and for religious novelty. It is the desire for religious novelty that permits the Christians
to make good use of new forms of expression, such as the codex,
rather than the traditional scroll.[34] Those Christian thinkers whom
we can identify as radicals seek to abolish traditional social links.
The society they want to build is an ideal one, an anti-city, whose
model they will establish in the desert in the fourth century. These
new masters of wisdom teach, first of all, free of charge. Thus
Justin Martyr, describing his quest for a real school of wisdom
and truth in the first chapters of his *Dialogue with Trypho*, written before 150, rejects the Aristotelian philosopher because he will
teach only for a fee. The teaching of true wisdom should be free
of charge and offered to all equally. In this school of a new kind,
instead of tuition fees, a total commitment is demanded of the
student, entailing a radical break with the world of the city, the
realm of ideas as well as of passions. This is not to say that there
was no existential commitment in philosophical schools, where
one also had to choose a way of living. But for the philosophers,

---

33. See Veyne in *Sénèque, Entretiens*, 596. When Origen is expelled from Alexandria
by Bishop Demetrios, his whole "School of Advanced Religious Studies," as Marrou
calls it, collapses. Marrou, *The History of Education*, part 2, 145.

34. See Guy G. Stroumsa, "Early Christianity: A Religion of the Book?" in *Homer,
the Bible, and Beyond: Literary and Religious Canons in Ancient Societies*, ed. Margalit
Finkelberg and Guy G. Stroumsa, Jerusalem Studies in Religion and Culture, no. 2
(Leiden: Brill, 2003), 153–74.

this way of living permitted them to devote themselves to a life of ideas, to epistemological reflection. For the first Christian thinkers, and for the desert fathers after them in the fourth century, philosophy is already (long before the medieval scholastics) *ancilla theologiae*. Even more powerfully, Theodoretus will be able to say in the fifth century (in Marxist fashion, as it were) that while the Greek philosophers offered explanations of the world, the monks, the new philosophers, propose to change it.

It is thus a new kind of wisdom that Christian thinkers, from Paul on, offer: a paradoxical wisdom, foolishness for the wise of this world (I Cor. 1:18). The first Christian teachers are often martyrs, like Justin Martyr, Pionios (called *didaskalos*), or Origen. Hence the importance of Socrates in patristic literature, a figure well studied by Adolf von Harnack long ago.

It has often been said that the Christian school of Alexandria claimed to be a philosophical school.[35] At least, it appeared to be one, as Christian thinkers wanted to offer a legitimate alternative to Hellenic intellectuals. But the wisdom they sought is of quite a different nature, and so were the ways of seeking it: *sōtēria* is the goal much more than *epistēmē*. To be sure, they did comment on texts (biblical texts rather than those of Plato or Aristotle), but the aim was to put them into practice in order to be saved. The new wisdom was less dialectical than apodictic in nature. This transformation goes a long way to explaining the development of the literary genre of apophthegms among the monks.

"Speak a word to me, that I be saved." This phrase of the *Apophthegmata Patrum* encapsulates the role of the Christian teacher: he is the one who permits his disciple, the monk, enrolled and totally involved in the new school, to achieve his goal of personal salvation. The nature of the teacher's word is no longer explanatory, putting the disciple on the track of intellectual autonomy.

---

35. See Robert L. Wilken, "Alexandria: A School for Training in Virtue," in *Schools of Thought in the Christian Tradition*, ed. Patrick Henry (Philadelphia: Fortress Press, 1984), 15–30.

This word has acquired quite a different authority and power. The role of the Christian teacher is thus quite different from that of the philosopher, the teacher of wisdom. He does not guide his disciple only in order to let him follow his own way, but accompanies him in his quest for salvation until he reaches his goal. His role is no longer contingent. He is no longer someone simply more advanced along the path, whose teaching helps the disciple. The term "spiritual master" refers not only to a vague spirituality, but rather to his different mode of activity. The new wisdom is anti-intellectual by nature, as shown by the transformation of the concept of *logismos*. In the literature stemming from the monastic milieus, even with an intellectual like Evagrius Ponticus, *logismoi* have become evil thoughts (all thoughts are evil!) that invade the monk's mind, preventing him from reaching salvation. The goal of the spiritual master, then, is to chase these thoughts away, to prevent the disciple from thinking for himself. On the other hand, one must insist on the central role of the conflict with demons in ascetic life. In monastic literature, this conflict is a real metaphor of ascetic life.[36] We should note the radical transformation effected since the time of the Greco-Roman teacher of wisdom. The power of the spiritual master upon his disciple now seems to be total. One can follow the emergence and development of the new form of authority being developed among the monks.[37] This new pattern of authority is parallel to that of the bishop, with which it sometimes conflicts.

Prima facie, this transformation of spiritual authority may look surprising in a religion established on evangelical *logoi* such as "Call no one your father on earth" (Matt. 23:9). And yet, the desert fathers, heirs to the Pharisian fathers, have an authority that the Pharisians, like the philosophers, never had. This au-

36. See David Brakke, "The Making of Monastic Demonology: Three Ascetic Teachers on Withdrawal and Resistance," *Church History* 70 (2001): 19–48.

37. See Philip Rousseau, *Ascetics, Authority, and the Church in the Age of Jerome and Cassian* (Oxford: Oxford University Press, 1978), 21–32. See further Graham Gould, *The Desert Fathers on Monastic Community* (Oxford: Clarendon Press, 1993), chap. 2, "The Abba and His Disciple."

thority stems from the fact that there is almost no knowledge to communicate, nor methods of thinking to teach. Even the sacred texts are not necessarily perceived as texts to be mastered. Athanasius's *Life of Antony*, for instance, perhaps the most influential Christian text after the New Testament, reflects an attitude of deep ambiguity toward the study of Scripture. In his discussion of what monks must know about Scripture, Abba Isaiah of Gaza praises ignorance (*agnoia*), which draws the monk near God (6.1). Antony becomes in the desert "a father for the monks in the surrounding areas."[38] Utterances of the Christian fathers have obtained a quasi-magical power, ensuring salvation on the spot. The spiritual director is less a sage than a saint.[39] In this sense, he is the image of divine perfection. The evangelical injunction to "Be perfect, as your heavenly Father is perfect!" (Matt. 5:48) can be followed through the imitation of the saint, the intermediary model. Perhaps the clearest example of the spiritual master's new function is that of Barsanuphius in the desert of Gaza. His letters constitute the richest corpus of the literary genre of spiritual direction, to which I shall only allude here, as it is presently being studied from various viewpoints. Lorenzo Perrone, for instance, has recently called attention to the suppression of will and the importance of the master's advice, as they are reflected in the correspondence between Barsanuphius and John of Gaza. Perrone notes the fact that in the ancient monastic system of spiritual direction, pedagogical experience informs the whole life of the master as well as the disciple's.[40]

This paradox—namely, the relative weakness of knowledge in the new teaching—is not easily explained. And yet I cannot but

38. Athanasius of Alexandria, *Life of Antony*, trans. Tim Vivian and Apostolos N. Athanassakis (Kalamazoo, MI: Cistercian Press, 2003).

39. See, for instance, Douglas Burton-Christie, *The Word in the Desert: Scripture and the Quest for Holiness in Early Christian Monasticism* (New York: Oxford University Press, 1993).

40. Lorenzo Perrone, "The Necessity of Advice: Spiritual Direction as a School of Christianity in the Correspondence of Barsanuphius and John of Gaza," in *Christian Gaza in Late Antiquity*, ed. Brouria Bitton-Ashkelony and Aryeh Kofsky (Leiden: Brill, 2004), 131–50.

ask myself if the new power of Christian speech does not origi-
nate in the religious structures of Christianity. For these structures, almost unknown elsewhere in the ancient world, there is
no salvation except through an intermediary, a *mesitēs*, a master
at once human and divine. Another evangelical statement justi-
fies the great power of the master as disciple of Jesus: "Whoever
listens to you listens to me!" (Luke 10:16). As is well shown, for
instance, in the texts of Dorotheus of Gaza, the desert master
relays the divine master, as prefigured by Moses (see Gregory of
Nyssa's *Life of Moses*). For Dorotheus, the spiritual master must
destroy self-confidence in his disciple: "He lived in the monas-
tery for five years, without having ever done his own will, in any
way, or having been moved by passion."[41]

Obedience to the spiritual father, however, does not simply
mean submission to authority, but is established upon faith, trust,
and love.[42] This explains why the pagan teacher of wisdom has
absolutely no need of a disciple; he can return at any time to his
personal reflection and abandon humanity to its fate. The Christian spiritual master, on the other hand, is closely tied to his disciples from an existential point of view. He is worth as much,
or as little, as they are, and his own salvation depends on theirs.
Abba Isaiah explains to his disciples that if they practice his pre-
cepts, he will speak to God on their behalf. If they do not, however, God will not only ask them to account for their negligence,
but will also accuse Isaiah of being useless.[43] John Cassian, who
carried to the West the methods and the goals of Eastern monasticism, tells us similar things: "My sons, it is your zeal which
led me to speak for so long. Because of your eagerness, some kind
of fire has given a more urgent sense to what I have been saying."

41. Dorotheus of Gaza, *Discourses and Sayings*, trans. Eric Wheeler (Kalamazoo, MI:
Cistercian Press, 1977).

42. As pointed out by Jean-Claude Larchet, *Thérapeutique des maladies spirituelles:
Une introduction à la tradition ascétique de l'Eglise orthodoxe* (Paris: Cerf, 1997). Larchet
insists on the therapeutic role of the spiritual father.

43. Isaiah of Scetis, *Ascetikon*, Logos 1, in *Ascetic Discourses*, trans. John Chryssavgis
and Pachomios Penkett (Kalamazoo, MI: Cistercian Press, 2002).

And again: "For the more insistent your demand, the greater the care I owe to your faith."[44]

This phenomenological analysis of the relationship between teacher and disciple has dealt with only some of its aspects. But it exemplifies the true transformation of the status of the self in Late Antiquity. This transformation, which came with the victory of Christianity, upset the relationship between master and disciple as it was known among Jewish and pagan sages alike. Recognition of such a transformation means that we do not see in Evagrius simply "a philosopher in the desert," as Antoine Guillaumont has called him.[45] For Evagrius, Gnostic teaching has only one goal (a goal ignored by the philosopher): he must teach salvation.[46] Even as deep a thinker with as independent a mind as Evagrius, then, remains foremost a spiritual master. It is only metaphorically that one can still speak of "master of wisdom." With the conversion of the empire to Christianity, we witness a real transformation of the relationship between teacher and disciple, at least in monastic milieus, where the parting of the ways of cultural traditions prevails over continuity. The historical paradox, then, is that it is precisely the monastic movement that would be the main bearer of the ancient intellectual heritage into the Middle Ages.

44. John Cassian, *Conferences*, trans. Colm Luibheid (New York: Paulist Press, 1985), 1.23, p. 58, and 2.1, p. 60.

45. See Antoine Guillaumont, "Evagre le Pontique: Un philosophe au désert," in *Aux origines du monachisme chrétien*, Spiritualité orientale, no. 30 (Bégrolles-en-Mauge: Abbaye de Bellefontaine, 1979), 185–212. On spiritual direction in Evagrius, see Gabriel Bunge, *Paternité spirituelle: La gnose chrétienne chez Evagre le Pontique*, Spiritualité orientale, no. 60 (Bégrolles en Mauge: Abbaye de Bellefontaine, 1994).

46. Evagrius of Ponticus, *The Greek Ascetic Corpus*, trans. and ed. Robert E. Sinkewicz (New York: Oxford University Press, 2003).

Conclusion

I subtitled this volume *Religious Transformations in Late Antiquity*. I have tackled here five of them and only treated some of their aspects. There are of course others. One might without difficulty study the transformations of mythology, magic, esoterism, hierarchical and ecclesiastical authority, philosophical thought, artistic representation, and literary creation, showing how their very status was radically changed in Late Antiquity. Then one would show how along with these transformations came forms of religious and cultural heritage—not from "Europe" (an overused term that too often still means Western Europe of Catholic and Protestant tradition), but from the three civilizations of which we are all the heirs: alongside Latin Europe, that of Byzantium, from Constantinople to Moscow ("the third Jerusalem"), and that of Islam, from Baghdad to Cordoba. Byzantium and Islam end up transmitting to neo-Latin Europe, with a long delay, a portion of their ancient heritages.[1] These are commonplaces, of course, but are nevertheless often forgotten. I have just mentioned the three great cultural and religious axes—which are not *las tres culturas* bandied about today by the Spanish tourist office. The Jews, in medieval Spain as elsewhere, were represented on

---

1. See Rémi Brague, *Europe, la voie romaine* (Paris: Criterion, 1992).

both sides in military clashes and other power struggles, which undoubtedly enabled them to serve as mediators between cultures.

I had begun this journey with the hypothesis of the capital importance of religious transformations in Late Antiquity, but without prejudging what I would find and without trying to present a rigid theory accounting for the complex transformation of structures in history. It is only now, looking back at the theses I developed here, that I become aware of the particular place held in my discourse by Judaism. The Jews seem to be at the origin of each of the transformations I have studied: personal identity, the place of the Book, the abandoning of sacrifices, the development of communities—Judaism seems to have experimented before other religious systems with all these aspects of the "new" religion that emerges in Late Antiquity.

Speaking of mutations—as I did, in the French original version of this book, to describe religious transformations—is to think of Darwin, of the strange discoveries during his voyage on the *Beagle*, which would eventually result in 1859 in *On the Origin of Species* and of the concept of survival of the fittest. More than a generation ago, the English historian Arnold Toynbee wrote of the Jews that they were a "fossil" conserving in a frozen way a previous state of civilization. People were justly scandalized by Toynbee's expression, seeing it as an insult to a people who tried literally to rise from its own ashes. But if one amends Toynbee's metaphor and imagines a living, active fossil—certainly an oxymoron—one might perhaps find one conclusion to this volume.

To conclude, I would like briefly to take up one of the questions I posed at the beginning: Ancient Christianity or Late Antiquity? In other words, should we conceive of ancient Christianity as the bearer, or rather as the creator, of the mutations we have detected? Our observations might bring an answer to this question: it is in large part thanks to its Jewish heritage that Christianity was able to invent new frameworks in which religion would redefine itself.

As we have just seen, these frameworks would also remain for too long those of religious intolerance. It was only at the beginning of the modern era, in a Christian Europe torn by religious violence, that a solution started to take shape: for John Locke and Pierre Bayle, tolerance—the very word makes its appearance only in Locke's *De tolerantia* in 1689—implied recognition of the fact that if faith is subjective, it is subject to error and does not reflect a perfect match with truth. Finally, we have perceived in modern times the emergence of the right to *falsa religio* that is being asserted. Locke's principal argument was founded on the distinction between the political framework and the religious community, that is to say, on the separation between Church and State. Today this is still the sole possible basis of peaceful relations in our multi-religious societies.

Index of Names